"Mike Emlet has written
fall into extreme position
are suffering. Approach
for Scripture is quite cle
do not really even understand ourselves! I pray this book will bear the
fruit of humility and compassion in God's people."

Diane Langberg, Psychologist; author of *Suffering and the Heart of God*

"Mike Emlet has written a much-needed book on psychiatric diagnosis from a biblical worldview. Humbly admitting we have to grow in our understanding of biological issues that interplay with spiritual struggles is right. Challenging a reductionist biological view of man is also right. It is time for the biblical counseling movement to adopt a more robust, balanced, and holistic approach to caring for those who suffer most. This book goes a long way to help us turn the corner. I highly recommend it."

Garrett Higbee, Executive Director of Biblical Soul Care for Harvest Bible Chapel; founding board member of the Biblical Counseling Coalition; president of Soul Care Consulting

"In the midst of all the conflicting voices in our culture about psychiatric diagnoses and psychotropic medications, Dr. Michael Emlet has provided a helpful gift to the church. In this short book, you'll find a clear and nuanced discussion of the wisdom of using or not using psychiatric descriptions and medications. Recognizing the uniqueness of each situation, Dr. Emlet will assist you in making the best decision for each case by furnishing a framework that isn't the same with every person. I'm thankful for it."

Elyse M. Fitzpatrick, Author of *Will Medicine Stop the Pain?*

"Mike Emlet brings up a topic at the dinner table that most people couldn't—at least not without causing indigestion. You will find Emlet the best kind of conversationalist on a difficult topic like psychiatric medications, making distinctions clear when needed and acknowledging mystery when needed. This book is instantly in my curriculum."

Jeremy Pierre, Associate Professor of Biblical Counseling, The Southern Baptist Theological Seminary; author of *The Dynamic Heart in Daily Life: Connecting Christ to Human Experience*

"The intersection of ministry, mental health, and medicine is the Bermuda Triangle of soul care. Dr. Emlet applies his unique multidisciplinary training to cut through mystery, myth, and, misconception. Biblical wisdom is the compass to navigate these troubled waters. *Descriptions & Prescriptions* leans into Scripture as it rejoices in appreciation for God's gift of medical treatment and holistic pastoral care."

Stephen P. Greggo, Professor of Counseling, Trinity Evangelical Divinity School; coeditor of *Counseling and Christianity: Five Approaches*

"Counselors have needed direction on navigating the struggles of the human brain and soul, while neither dismissing labeling completely nor fully embracing hook, line, and sinker, everything taught in modern psychiatry. Mike Emlet has again given us wise counsel from the Bible, utilizing his medical background to clarify the language of labeling and the wise use of medication."

Rod Mays, National Staff, Reformed University Fellowship; adjunct faculty, Reformed Theological Seminary

"As a pastor and counselor, it is hard not to be overwhelmed by the complexity of mental health struggles. Mike's book is like a new set of glasses, bringing clarity to these complex issues. Without giving all the answers, Mike lays out perceptive pointers to help readers navigate difficult terrain. Whether you are a pastor, lay leader, parent, or a concerned friend, this book will provide you much needed wisdom."

Kurt Peters, Pastor of St Matthew's Anglican Church, Botany (Sydney); Director of Biblical Counseling Australia

"Mike has given us a balanced and reliable guide to psychiatric diagnoses and medical therapies from a biblical perspective that is well-informed by experience and science. Practical, clear, and perceptive, it will be helpful to pastors and mental health professionals, as well as those who suffer in the ways described in the *DSM-5*. In my opinion, this is the best book in its area for years."

Karl B. Hood, Lecturer in Pastoral Care, Presbyterian Theological College, Melbourne, Australia

"With a physician's training harnessed by Scripture, Mike Emlet leads us along the tightrope of psychiatric considerations with both a poise and grace not often seen when Christians approach this topic. Both the mental health practitioner and the pastoral counselor should be pleased with this robust analysis that challenges us all to rethink our categories in favor of a gospel-centered accounting of these post-fall realities."

John Applegate, Executive Director of the Philadelphia Renewal Network; psychiatrist and director of John Applegate, MD & Associates, LLC

"I recommend this book to help pastors and mature believers in the church who want to better understand the challenges of human psychological suffering from a gospel-centered perspective. Drawing on his personal experience with those who are afflicted by problems of mental health, Emlet leads us away from a reductionist approach to one that is holistic and includes both heart and body. His work gives us an excellent start in ministering to those who suffer."

François Turcotte, President of Séminaire Baptiste Évangélique du Québec (SEMBEQ); elder at Église Baptiste du Plateau Mont-Royal

"The relationship between the spheres of the medical and the spiritual in pastoral care can be an extremely tricky one to navigate, especially for pastors with no medical training. That is why this clear and concise book by Mike Emlet is so important. He eschews the simple reductionism of approaches that deny any usefulness to psychiatric medication, while also refusing to eliminate the spiritual component in many psychiatric disorders. This is a small book but one that should be on the shelf of all those involved in pastoral care."

Carl R. Trueman, Author; pastor, Cornerstone Presbyterian Church, Ambler, PA

"Any book that has 'A Biblical Perspective on Psychiatric Diagnoses and Medications' in its subtitle is going to be huge, complex, impractical, and highly controversial. Right? Wrong! Mike Emlet has managed to write a short, accessible, and immensely practical book on this vital subject. And he's done it in such a sensible, balanced, and biblical way that the book will promote peace and unity rather than debate and division. Here is help for the helpers and for the helpless."

David Murray, Professor of Old Testament and Practical Theology at Puritan Reformed Theological Seminary; pastor of Grand Rapids Free Reformed Church; author of *Reset: Living a Grace-Paced Life in a Burnout Culture*

"In *Descriptions and Prescriptions*, Michael R. Emlet makes accessible for the lay Christian otherwise technical information about the symptoms and treatments of psychiatric disorders. He presents these issues within a biblical anthropology and seeks to help move Christians beyond a generalized fear of psychiatric illnesses and treatments to a 'third way' between solely spiritualizing or over-medicalizing these illnesses."

Kathryn Greene-McCreight, Author of *Darkness Is My Only Companion: A Christian Response to Mental Illness*

"As a Christian, have you ever wondered how to think about psychiatric labels and medications? Dr. Michael Emlet has provided a thoughtful, balanced, biblical approach to diagnoses and medications in this book. I'm planning to buy copies and give this out to many of our members."

Deepak Reju, Pastor of Biblical Counseling and Family Ministry, Capitol Hill Baptist Church, Washington, DC; author of *The Pastor and Counseling* and *She's Got the Wrong Guy*

"Because our culture increasingly describes problems in terms of psychiatric diagnoses and increasingly seeks solutions through psychoactive medications, this is a vital book for our times. We all need to think more carefully about the labels we are using and the drugs we are taking. This will become a go-to book for Christians wanting a balanced, biblical, and compassionate view of the descriptions and prescriptions that psychiatrists use."

Steve Midgley, Executive Director, Biblical Counseling UK

"Michael Emlet has nailed it! Finally, we have a medically informed and biblically wise approach regarding what we really know and don't know about psychiatric diagnoses and medications. We need this holistic aim in ministering to spiritual, emotional, and biological care for those who are suffering. This book is both fascinating and succinct and I will be recommending it often."

Aimee Byrd, author of *Housewife Theologian*, *Theological Fitness*, and *No Little Women*

"A reference book of great value for caregivers, particularly those of us who are not medical professionals. Mike skilfully deals with a very complex issue and provides a balanced view of the advantages and limitations of 'descriptions' and 'prescriptions' as well as the important role of biblical counselling in the overall healing process. A must read for secular and biblical counsellors alike."

John K. John, Director, Biblical Counseling Trust of India

DESCRIPTIONS AND PRESCRIPTIONS:

A BIBLICAL PERSPECTIVE ON PSYCHIATRIC DIAGNOSES AND MEDICATIONS

Michael R. Emlet

New
Growth
Press

newgrowthpress.com

New Growth Press, Greensboro, NC 27404
newgrowthpress.com

Cover Design: Faceout Books, faceoutstudio.com
Typesetting and eBook: Lisa Parnell, lparnell.com

ISBN 978-1-945270-11-6 (Print)
ISBN 978-1-945270-12-3 (eBook)

Library of Congress Cataloging-in-Publication Data

Names: Emlet, Michael R., author.
Title: Descriptions and prescriptions : a biblical perspective on psychiatric
  diagnoses and medications / Michael R. Emlet.
Description: Greensboro, NC : New Growth Press, [2017] | Includes index.
Identifiers: LCCN 2017036019 | ISBN 9781945270116 (trade paper)
Subjects: LCSH: Psychiatry and religion. | Psychiatry--Diagnosis--Religious
  aspects--Christianity. | Psychiatry--Treatment--Religious
  aspects--Christianity.
Classification: LCC RC455.4.R4 E45 2017 | DDC 616.89--dc23
LC record available at https://lccn.loc.gov/2017036019

Printed in India

28 27 26 25 24 23 22 21   3 4 5 6 7

To those I know
who have struggled with mental illness
but have endeavored not to be defined by it

CONTENTS

Introduction

THE GOLDILOCKS PRINCIPLE

What do you think when someone you know is diagnosed with a psychiatric disorder? Or has started to take a psychoactive medication? Do you say to yourself, "Finally, he is getting the help he really needs!" Or do you feel skeptical about either the diagnosis or the solution (or both), and wonder if what the person really needs is simply to trust in Jesus more?

It doesn't take too many conversations in the church to realize that there are widely divergent views regarding the diagnosis and treatment of mental health issues. Like many, you may find yourself falling into one of two camps. Let me call this the Goldilocks Principle. What do I mean?

You may be one who is "too cold" toward psychiatric diagnoses. You're highly suspicious of using these labels. You believe that they are secular understandings of the person that compete with biblical categories and solutions. At best you don't think they're helpful, and at worst you believe they are harmful and dehumanizing.

Or perhaps you are "too warm" toward psychiatric diagnoses. You may embrace them as nearly all-encompassing explanations of the person's struggle. You may gravitate toward medical solutions and diminish the relevance of the biblical story for these particular problems. But is there a third way, a balance between these two extreme tendencies?

Similarly, you may be "too cold" toward psychoactive medications. You're extremely wary of ever using them. If you're honest, you believe that Christians really wouldn't have to take psychiatric medication if their faith were robust enough. And what about those side effects—why risk it?

Or you may be among those who are "too warm" toward psychoactive medications. If a Christian has no problem using Tylenol for a headache, why shouldn't she use an antidepressant when she is depressed? And about those side effects—they are invariably worth the benefit. But is there a third way, a balance between these two extreme tendencies?

One goal of this short book is to help you move from either extreme—too cold or too hot—toward a view of psychiatric diagnoses and medications that is hopefully "just right." Perhaps you *don't* tend toward one of these extremes but you are looking for the biblical and scientific framework that allows you to maintain that third-way position. That's exactly what I hope this material will do. I want to take seriously what help psychiatric categories and medications provide but also recognize their limitations.

There is no doubt that many people suffer greatly with emotions and patterns of thinking that bring grave hardship to them and to their loved ones. The pressing issue is how best to know and understand their struggles. And then, having understood, how best to provide compassionate and wise help. After all, we are called to "bear one another's burdens and so fulfill the law of Christ" (Galatians 6:2). Psychiatric diagnostic classification and psychoactive medications provide a way to understand and help those who are burdened in particular ways. This book assesses the limitations and benefits of understanding and helping people using that lens.

I am writing this resource primarily for helpers in the church—pastors, counselors, elders, deacons, youth workers, men's and women's ministry coordinators, small group leaders, and other wise people who may not have a formal title or ministry job description but are actively engaged as intentional friends in one-another ministry. You are on the front lines of pastoral care and, no doubt, you have cared for and will continue to minister to people who struggle with mental anguish, who are diagnosed with psychiatric disorders, and who may be using or have questions about psychoactive medications.

If you are suffering with some form of mental illness and have received a diagnosis, I want to make certain that you don't hear any evaluation I provide of the psychiatric diagnostic system as a critique of your personal experience. For some of you, receiving a diagnosis illuminated your struggle and brought much-needed treatment. For others of you, a diagnosis may not have served you as well or was associated with unhelpful treatment. Please hear me when I say that my goal is to more fully humanize your struggle by pointing out what psychiatric diagnoses tell us—and don't tell us—about people. God says that you are "fearfully and wonderfully made" (Psalm 139:14) and I take that interpretive lens on your life seriously.

You will notice that I have many footnotes. While I don't want to be overly technical, I think it is important with a subject this complex to support my assertions and to discuss nuances when there is a need. However, I also want this material to be useful and bear fruit in real life ministry situations; it should not simply exist as a reference work. So feel free to skip the footnotes as you're reading if it helps to maintain the flow of the argument. You can come back to the notes later if you're interested in a greater level of detail.

This resource is in no way meant to be a comprehensive guide to helping those diagnosed with a mental illness, nor will it discuss the multifaceted approaches that exist for helping those who are suffering in this way. I simply want to provide a foundational biblical framework for understanding psychiatric diagnoses (Part 1) and the use of psychoactive medications (Part 2). Ultimately, I want this book to help you to think wisely and compassionately about these struggles so that you are just a bit more equipped for this important work of burden-bearing and counseling.

Part 1: Understanding Psychiatric Diagnoses

Chapter 1

DIAGNOSIS IS UNAVOIDABLE

Everybody "makes" diagnoses. Everybody. Interpreting—or diagnosing—our experiences is unavoidable. Part of being human is classifying, organizing, and interpreting our world. This is an echo of God's "organizing" speech, as he created something meaningful out of chaos (Genesis 1). As God created, he named day and night, heavens, earth, and the seas. Then he allowed Adam to name the creatures that filled the days and nights, the heavens, earth, and seas. God's image bearers were to "rule over" the earth in his stead and under his authority (Genesis 1:28). Before the fall this was done in dependence upon God. But after the fall, apart from God's grace, we function as autonomous interpreters and organizers of our world, without reference to God.

When it comes to some classification schemes, the stakes are not very high because they are not tied to the way we understand human beings—for example, it's not that critical when we classify music into genres of rock, punk, classical, jazz, country, and R & B. Other classification systems get closer to our identity, such as those marking out race and ethnicity. Still other classifications get even closer to our fundamental nature as image bearers and worshipers of God: sinner, sufferer, victim, oppressor, addict, adulterer, etc. The psychiatric classification system used by mental health professionals in the United States is one such important schema. How we understand one another is critical. Error here means misunderstanding at best and personal catastrophe at worst.

Psychiatrist Peter Kramer rightly noted, "How we see a person is a function of the categories we recognize—of our own private diagnostic system."[1] For example, let's say that after meeting a person for the first time you "diagnose" that person as "odd" or perhaps less charitably as a "self-oriented, insensitive jerk." What if you found out later that this person had been diagnosed with "autism spectrum disorder"? Do you modify your view of the person and his actions in light of this alternate diagnostic scheme? Perhaps in some ways yes, and others, no. But either way, you see how the nature of "the diagnosis" suggests a particular view of the person and possible responses to that person.

We want our classification schemes to match the nature of reality. That is, we want to use valid categories. No one wants to be misdiagnosed, whether using biblical language or secular language. We want the words and categories we use to mean something, to be revelatory about the way things really are.

Consider this list of diagnostic categories: Alzheimer's disease, bipolar disorder, alcohol withdrawal, pedophilic disorder, attention-deficit/hyperactivity disorder, obsessive-compulsive disorder, antisocial personality disorder, autism spectrum disorder, and borderline personality disorder. They all represent diagnoses found in psychiatry's standard reference text—*The Diagnostic and Statistical Manual of Mental Disorders*, better known as the *DSM*.[2]

In light of what I've said so far, it's appropriate to raise multiple questions: How do we understand the nature of psychiatric

---

1. Peter D. Kramer, *Listening to Prozac* (New York: Penguin Books, 1997), 68.
2. *The Diagnostic and Statistical Manual of Mental Disorders,* 5ᵗʰ Edition [*DSM-5*] (Arlington, VA: American Psychiatric Association, 2013).

diagnoses? What do these diagnoses mean? Are they all equally valid? How much information do they truly provide about the person? Is it wise for Christians to use these secular categories, and, if so, how? How should they shape the way we minister to persons who come to us with such diagnoses? Do we need to become "bilingual"? That is, do we need to become fluent in using *DSM* categories as well as biblical ones if we want to be truly helpful to others? Are psychiatric diagnostic categories antithetical to and in competition with biblical categories? Parallel to biblical categories? Overlapping with biblical categories in some way?

These questions are important, particularly in our time and place. The language of psychiatric diagnosis is not only known within the mental health world but is commonly used within the general population as well. Terms such as OCD, PTSD, and ADHD are part of our culture in formal and informal ways. So we can't afford to keep our heads in the sand with a dismissive and isolationist posture. Nor can we afford simply to accept the entire psychiatric diagnostic enterprise at face value. We need a balanced, biblically (and scientifically!) informed approach that is neither too warmly embracing nor too coldly dismissive. Striking this balance is important. This is not just an academic discussion within the walls of training institutions for pastors, counselors, psychiatrists, and other physicians. Consider what potentially happens as you move toward the extremes I mentioned in the introduction.

Let's say you are "too warm" toward psychiatric diagnoses. What might that look like in practice if a person recently diagnosed with bipolar disorder came to your church or small group? It might mean emphasizing medical care to the exclusion of pastoral care because physicians (psychiatrists) are understood as the experts here. It could lead to overlooking broader biblical categories and themes for understanding and helping the person, including identifying and addressing issues of suffering, shame, guilt, sin, and responsibility. Bottom line: You will point to incomplete solutions. You will miss ministry opportunities. Your approach to the person is truncated.

What if you are "too cold" toward psychiatric diagnoses? What could that stance look like in practice with a person diagnosed with bipolar disorder? You may have a skeptical, anti-psychiatry posture that is off-putting to the person and inhibits building a relationship. You will be more likely to see his problems only as sin—as something he does—rather than as suffering or weakness he has to face. You may ignore potentially helpful physical components to the person's total care, including medication. Bottom line: You will point to incomplete solutions. You will miss ministry opportunities. Your approach to the person is truncated.

Do you see how high the stakes are? I want us to move away from these two tendencies and toward a wiser middle ground. To do that, we need to examine the nature of psychiatric diagnoses more carefully.

The ultimate goal here is neither to vilify nor vindicate the psychiatric diagnostic system but to *help* those who struggle with disordered thoughts, emotions, and behaviors. To the extent that using psychiatric terminology helps with that goal, we must be open to that help. To the extent that using psychiatric terminology hinders that goal, we must offer wise and gracious critique. In both cases a gospel-centered approach full of rich biblical counsel must remain foundational to the way we minister.

In Part 1 of this book we will examine how psychiatric problems are diagnosed. We'll then see that the current system of diagnosis is a relatively recent phenomenon as we consider a brief history of twentieth-century psychiatry. These reflections will set us up to understand both the limitations and the potential benefits of psychiatric diagnoses in the context of ministry.

Chapter 2

HOW ARE PSYCHIATRIC PROBLEMS DIAGNOSED?

Let's start with how psychiatric problems are diagnosed. Consider this statement:

> The line of demarcation between sanity and insanity, like that between health and disease, is sometimes so nebulous that it becomes exceedingly difficult to decide where one ends and the other begins. Is it not a matter of wonder, therefore, that differences of opinion should arise in this connection, particularly when the question of responsibility is raised?[1]

Amazingly, this quote comes not from the current op-ed page of *The New York Times* but from *The Journal of the American Medical Association (JAMA)* in 1904! Over one hundred years later, psychiatrists still wrestle with this dilemma: How do you differentiate the mentally well from the mentally ill?

Current psychiatric diagnoses in the *DSM* consist of sets of symptoms (self-reported by the patient) and signs (observed by the

---

1. *JAMA* 43 (1904):740-41.

clinician) that cluster together. This is in line with how any physician is trained to diagnose problems. Consider a simple medical example: A patient reports *symptoms* of runny nose, sore throat, cough, and right ear pain. In a physical exam, the physician notes the following *signs*: mild fever (100.8 F), clear discharge from the nose, mildly red throat but no exudate (pus), and a right eardrum that is red and immobile. Based on her clinical judgment, the physician considers these symptoms and signs and makes the diagnosis—upper respiratory infection with a right otitis media (ear infection). A psychiatrist conducts a diagnostic evaluation in the same way. To be sure, symptoms and signs of disordered mental states may be more challenging to assess and verify, but it would be a mistake to assume that all that matters in psychiatric diagnosis is what the patient tells you.

Mental health professionals use the *DSM* as their defining resource for describing, categorizing, and diagnosing mental disorders. The core approach of the *DSM* is that underlying the symptoms and signs lies a greater whole, a specific diagnosis that ties the person's presentation together in a valid and meaningful way.

The American Psychiatric Association (APA) considers a "mental disorder" to be:

a syndrome characterized by clinically significant disturbance in an individual's cognition, emotion regulation, or behavior that reflects a dysfunction in the psychological, biological, or developmental processes underlying mental functioning. Mental disorders are usually associated with significant distress or disability in social, occupational, or other important activities. An expectable or culturally approved response to a common stressor or loss, such as the death of a loved one, is not a mental disorder. Socially deviant behavior (e.g., political, religious, or sexual) and conflicts that are primarily between the individual and society are not mental disorders unless the deviance or conflict results from a dysfunction in the individual as described above.[2]

Notice the emphases on distress, disability, and deviance. Also notice the categories of cognition, emotion, and behavior, which in Scripture are all reflective of our moral-spiritual lives before God.[3] These general ideas are fleshed out in the specifics of each diagnosis. For now, it's important to recognize that there are no laboratory tests or radiological studies (e.g., CT, PET, or MRI scans) that are generally used to arrive at diagnoses. For the vast majority of psychiatric diagnoses, the patient's self-report of his symptoms and the psychiatrist's observations of the person are the foundation of the diagnostic enterprise.

One exception, of course, would be a laboratory test (blood, urine) that confirms (for example) the presence of marijuana as part of making the *DSM* diagnosis of "cannabis intoxication," as would be true for other substances of abuse. Another exception would be the *DSM* diagnosis of narcolepsy, which has a test for hypocretin deficiency as part its criteria.[4] Additional research studying the usefulness of other tests for particular diagnoses continues, but those tests are not currently used in official diagnostic capacities.

---

2. *DSM*-5, 20.
3. For an extended discussion of how Scripture views our thinking, affection, emotions, will, and behavior as moral-spiritual faculties (i.e. reflective of our relationship with God), see Michael R. Emlet, "Understanding the Influences on the Human Heart," *The Journal of Biblical Counseling* 20, no. 2 (2002): 47-52.
4. *DSM*-5, 372-373.

Chapter 3

HOW DID WE GET HERE? A BRIEF HISTORY OF PSYCHIATRIC DIAGNOSIS

The fact that the *DSM* has had five major editions tells us that we didn't get here overnight. The evolution of the psychiatric diagnostic system occurred over time, but over a relatively short time. To understand the nature of modern psychiatric diagnosis, you need to understand a battle of two ideologies within psychiatry: psychodynamic psychiatry and biologically-oriented (descriptive) psychiatry.[1] A brief tour of the battlefield will help you appreciate what happened between 1952, when the *DSM-I* was published, and 2013, when the *DSM-5* was unveiled.

Before the twentieth century, there were only a few diagnostic categories when it came to mental health. Only the most severely afflicted were considered mentally ill; they manifested the modern-day equivalents of schizophrenia or bipolar disorder (manic-depression) and were generally housed in asylums. The *sine qua non* of mental illness was the presence of psychosis, a break from

---

1. See T. M. Luhrmann, *Of Two Minds: An Anthropologist Looks at American Psychiatry* (New York: Vintage, 2001). David Powlison notes that the battle between psychological and biological understandings of the person has been going on since the mid-1800s. See "Biological Psychiatry," *The Journal of Biblical Counseling* 17, no. 3 (1999): 2-8. Also see Alan V. Horwitz, *Creating Mental Illness* (Chicago: University of Chicago Press, 2002).

reality accompanied by hallucinations (sensory experiences not shared by others), delusions (fixed irrational beliefs), or both. Melancholy (severe depression) was also a widely recognized affliction.

Psychodynamic psychiatry had its origins with Freud in the early part of the twentieth century, and it became the dominant voice in American psychiatry in the 1950s-1970s. A psychodynamic approach favored a spectrum view of mental illness, saying that all mental illness exists on a spectrum between normal and abnormal. As Karl Menninger said, "Instead of putting so much emphasis on different kinds and clinical pictures of illness, we propose to think of all forms of mental illness as being essentially the same in quality and differing quantitatively."[2] So in this conception, schizophrenia would be a much more severe form of illness than "anxiety neurosis," but both diagnoses are on the same spectrum. Both problems would find their origin in anxiety arising from conflict within the individual's unconscious, intensified by social/environmental factors.

By using this theoretical orientation, increasing numbers of people fell into the category of "mentally ill" (having some kind of "neurosis").[3] The goal of treatment was to get behind the symptom and address its psychogenic (originating in the mind) cause. From this perspective arose the *DSM-I* (1952) and the *DSM-II* (1968). The problem is this: If everyone is on a spectrum, where does one draw the lines between well and unwell? Over time the failure of psychodynamic psychiatry to reliably differentiate these two groups opened the door to descriptive psychiatry.[4]

Descriptive psychiatrists generally had biologically-oriented views regarding the origin of mental problems. This was fueled

---

2. Mitchell Wilson, "DSM-III and the Transformation of American Psychiatry: A History," *American Journal of Psychiatry* 150, no. 3 (1993): 400.

3. See Horwitz, *Creating Mental Illness*, 38-55.

4. One particularly egregious example of this failure in both reliability and validity was reported by Charles Rosenhan, "On Being Sane in Insane Places," *Science* 179 (1973): 250-258.

in part by the success of the first antidepressants and antipsychotics developed in the late 1950s and beyond. Biochemical control of symptoms suggested the importance of exploring biochemical causes at the level of neurotransmission in the brain. These psychiatrists tended to have a discrete view of mental illness. That is, each mental illness should be viewed as a discrete, separate entity, and not on a spectrum. Unlike the psychodynamic conception, descriptive psychiatrists saw different mental illnesses as varying in both quality and quantity. Because they viewed one mental illness as significantly different from another, it became important to develop more stringent diagnostic criteria to differentiate the many problems in thinking and behavior observed by psychiatrists.

With the publication of the *DSM-III* in 1980, the descriptive approach triumphed. The psychodynamic language of *neurosis* and *reaction* was marginalized, and detailed lists of symptoms and signs were created for each diagnostic entity, many of which appeared for the first time. The focus was not on causation but on developing increasingly detailed descriptions for the growing number of problems psychiatrists encountered. Indeed, even the *DSM-5* says, "a diagnosis does not carry any necessary implications regarding the causes of the individual's mental disorder or the individual's degree of control over behaviors that may be associated with the disorder."[5] One impact on the diagnostic enterprise of focusing on description rather than causation has been the proliferation of psychiatric diagnoses from the *DSM-III* onward. Compared to the *DSM-I*, the *DSM-IV-TR* (the predecessor to the *DSM-5*) manifested a 300 percent increase in the number of diagnoses.[6]

Despite dissenting voices within mainstream psychiatry (see some examples below) and admissions within the *DSM-5* regarding

---

5. *DSM-5*, 25.

6. Arthur C. Houks, "Discovery, Invention, and the Expansion of the Modern *Diagnostic and Statistical Manuals of Mental Disorders*" in Larry E. Beutler and Mary L. Malik, eds., *Rethinking the DSM: A Psychological Perspective* (Washington, DC: American Psychological Association, 2002), 18.

the need for increased validity (correspondence to the real world)[7] in the diagnostic approach, it seems that the current descriptive system is here to stay for the foreseeable future. The framers of the *DSM-5* recognize the limitations of a descriptive or categorical system, but at this juncture do not have a more viable evidence-based alternative. Consider the following quotes from the *DSM-5*, which ironically show a pendulum shift back toward a "spectrum" model as a way to understand psychiatric disturbances (albeit with modern biological evidence driving the swing rather than psychodynamic theorizing): "Although some mental disorders may have well-defined boundaries around specific symptom clusters, scientific evidence now places many, if not most, disorders on a spectrum with closely related disorders that have shared symptoms, shared genetic and environmental risk factors, and possibly shared neural substrates [i.e. neurological underpinnings]. . . . *In short, we have come to recognize that the boundaries between disorders are more porous than originally perceived.*"[8] And so, "despite the problem posed by categorical [i.e., descriptive] diagnoses, the *DSM-5* Task Force recognized that it is premature scientifically to propose alternative definitions for most disorders."[9]

I have examined how psychiatric problems are diagnosed and have briefly surveyed the history of American psychiatry. Now let's look at the psychiatric diagnostic system in more depth. There are a number of concerns with the current approach to psychiatric diagnosis that many, even within the psychiatric community, have identified. I will point out four that I think merit the most attention. This will set us up in succeeding chapters to better assess both the limitations and the benefits of psychiatric categories in the context of interpersonal ministry.

---

7. For more details, including the distinction between reliability and validity, see Martyn Shuttleworth, "Definition of Reliability," https://explorable.com/definition-of-reliability.

8. *DSM-5*, 6 (emphasis mine).

9. *DSM-5*, 13.

Chapter 4

THE PROBLEMS AND PITFALLS OF PSYCHIATRIC DIAGNOSIS: DESCRIPTIONS, NOT EXPLANATIONS

The first point to address is this: *Psychiatric diagnoses are descriptions, not explanations.* Psychiatric diagnoses are descriptions of a person's thoughts, emotions, and behaviors, but not explanations for them.[1] They tell you *what* but not *why*. I'll spend the most time discussing this particular limitation.

Let me use a non-psychiatric problem to show you why this distinction is so important. Take a look at these manifestations of a common problem, one we have all struggled with:

- Red face
- Bulging veins at the temples
- Scowl
- Raised voice
- Hurtful words
- Clenched fists
- Stomping feet

---

1. See Edward T. Welch, *Blame it on the Brain? Distinguishing Chemical Imbalances, Brain Disorders, and Disobedience* (Phillipsburg, NJ: P & R, 1998).

What does this describe? Anger, of course! How can you tell that someone is angry? The person generally manifests some combination of the above characteristics. It's a good thing to reliably recognize that someone is angry! It *does* impact the way you approach the person.

But what if you saw me manifesting those "symptoms," rightly concluded that I was angry, and asked, "Why are you so angry?" And I respond, "I'm angry because I have a red face, I'm scowling, and I'm yelling." Would that answer your question? No! (*You* might get angry at that point!) That symptom list—red face, scowl, yelling—is a way to describe anger in more detail, but it doesn't say anything about *why* I'm angry. "Anger" is a one-word summary that is fleshed out in the details of the symptom list, but diagnosing me with "anger" based on the presence of those symptoms doesn't tell anyone *why* I'm angry. Now, how does this illustration concerning anger help us understand the way psychiatric diagnoses work?

As an example, let's look in detail at the diagnostic criteria for social phobia, better known as social anxiety disorder:[2]

- Marked fear or anxiety about one or more social situations in which the individual is exposed to possible scrutiny by others. Examples include social interactions (e.g., having a conversation, meeting unfamiliar people), being observed (e.g., eating or drinking), and performing in front of others (e.g., giving a speech).
- The individual fears that he or she will act in a way or show anxiety symptoms that will be negatively evaluated (i.e., will be humiliating or embarrassing; will lead to rejection or offend others).
- The social situations almost always provoke fear or anxiety.

2. *DSM-5*, 202-203.

- The social situations are avoided or endured with intense fear or anxiety.
- The fear or anxiety is out of proportion to the actual threat posed by the social situation and to the sociocultural context.
- The fear, anxiety, or avoidance is persistent, typically lasting for six months or more.
- The fear, anxiety, or avoidance causes clinically significant distress or impairment in social, occupational, or other important areas of functioning. [This criterion that the problem must significantly interfere with life is common to all the psychiatric diagnoses. That's one reason that, although many of us might identify to some degree with these symptoms, they don't rise to the level of a specific diagnosis, because they are not life-dominating. This should also serve as a guard to over-diagnosis.]
- The fear, anxiety, or avoidance is not due to the physiologic effects of a substance (e.g., a drug of abuse, a medication) or another medical condition. [This also is a criterion common to the diagnoses in the *DSM*. For example, if you were fine until you started a new blood pressure medication and now you are experiencing symptoms of extreme social anxiety, you would not be diagnosed with a mental illness; rather you might be judged to be suffering a medication side effect. The solution would be to discontinue the new medication under your physician's supervision to see what happens.]
- The fear, anxiety, or avoidance is not better explained by the symptoms of another mental disorder, such as panic disorder, body dysmorphic disorder, or autism spectrum disorder. [This criterion simply means that the person's symptoms do not better fit into another diagnostic category.]
- If another medical condition (e.g., Parkinson's disease, obesity, disfigurement from burns or injury) is present, the fear, anxiety, or avoidance is clearly unrelated or excessive. [This

criterion reminds the evaluator that other conditions may cause (or be expected to cause) anxiety or embarrassment in public, but the problem doesn't rise to the level of social anxiety disorder unless it is excessive.]

Notice that these criteria are all descriptive. In the same way we saw with anger, imagine asking your counselor or pastor, "Why do you think I have so much social anxiety?" and he or she responds, "Because you have marked fear or anxiety about one or more social situations in which you are exposed to possible scrutiny by others." Again, that's not very helpful, right? You've appropriately identified that there is a problem and what it looks like, but your ultimate goal is to understand *why* you are manifesting those symptoms.

You may be thinking, "Well, that's pretty obvious. But what's the problem? What's wrong with giving a name to a set of symptoms? Isn't this generally how the medical diagnostic system has historically evolved, by noticing symptoms and signs that tend to occur together, giving them a name and then developing plans to treat them?" The problem is this: Giving a label to a set of symptoms for an issue like social anxiety gives the *appearance* of precise explanation, but what kind of explanation is really being offered? In our medicalized and pharmacologically-driven culture, the average person often assumes that each diagnostic entity *is primarily caused* by a clear and specific brain dysfunction. But there is very little evidence to support that assumption. Lest I be misunderstood, there is an abundance of research that at the very least correlates (associates) symptoms in many psychiatric disorders with changes in brain imaging or other biochemical markers. But as I noted earlier, even the framers of the *DSM* do not consider this evidence strong enough to base a diagnosis on at this point.

At the same time, researchers at the NIMH (National Institute of Mental Health) are working on a classification scheme that will be thoroughly evidence-driven, based on the assumption that "mental disorders are biological disorders involving brain circuits that implicate specific domains of cognition, emotion, or behavior."[3] (Notice the difference from the *DSM-5* definition of a mental disorder I mentioned earlier.) They go on to say, "In short, the NIMH is trying to find a new categorization system that takes into account more of the biology, genetics, brain circuitry and neurochemistry that we've discovered in the past three decades' worth of research is becoming increasingly relevant to understanding mental disorders."[4]

What should we think of this? The use of "biomarkers" to consistently diagnose psychiatric disorders is likely years away and still won't resolve many questions of cause and treatment. For example, why are many forms of counseling (especially studied are cognitive-behavioral type therapies) associated with significant improvement in these NIMH-deemed "biological disorders"? How does counseling "work" compared with medication? Even if certain biomarkers are present in particular disorders, it is unlikely to mean that we have understood all factors that lead to the problem.

Even with psychiatric problems that run in families, have consistent brain imaging correlates, a predictable course and response to specific treatments (like schizophrenia), we must acknowledge the complex interaction of multiple factors—physical, spiritual, relational, situational, and cultural—that combine in causative ways for a given individual. Taking all of these factors into account is critical for providing the best care for struggling individuals.

Consider the analogy with other medical problems. This complex association of multiple factors exists for many, if not most, common medical ailments that clearly have an established biological cause. For example, there are strong genetic risk factors for hypertension (high blood pressure), but lifestyle decisions including diet and exercise play a huge role in determining whether someone develops hypertension.

---

3. John M. Grohol, "Did the NIMH Withdraw Support for the DSM? No," http://psychcentral.com/blog/archives/2013/05/07/did-the-nimh-withdraw-support-for-the-dsm-5-no/.
4. Ibid.

In a given person, one or more factors may predominate. In someone where biological factors predominate, a person may have high blood pressure and require medication even if a healthy diet and weight, low salt intake, and regular exercise are daily lifestyle choices. Others with no family history of hypertension but who overeat, consume a lot of salty, processed foods, and don't exercise may be diagnosed with high blood pressure as well. If this complexity is true for well-studied medical problems, how much more careful do we need to be in assigning a dominant cause in psychiatric disorders?

Nevertheless, this assumption of biological root cause is widespread within our culture and is fueled in part by pharmaceutical advertising. Consider, as an example, the text of an advertisement for the medication Zoloft, which is approved for social phobia:

> Social anxiety can be overwhelming. You might shake, sweat, or feel panicky. You may feel embarrassed when you are in a group. You may worry that you are being judged. You just feel so isolated. These are some signs of social anxiety disorder. It is a real medical condition that can get in the way of your daily life. The cause is not known. But it may happen when natural chemicals between the brain's nerve cells are out of balance. Prescription Zoloft works to correct this imbalance.[5]

Despite some of the internal ambiguities in the ad—"it is a real medical condition" yet "the cause is not known"—it captures a sufferer's experience well and suggests that the cause and cure of the malady is biological. The assumption of an ultimate biological cause for most psychiatric problems is enshrined in our culture, even if it is not viewed as a slam-dunk in academic and research-oriented psychiatry, which has a much more nuanced view involving nature and nurture.

Even the way we use the terms in conversation makes subtle assumptions. Notice the difference between saying, "I struggle with anxiety in social situations" vs. "I have social anxiety

5. *Ebony,* December 2003, 41.

disorder." The latter *suggests* an underlying biological cause, some kind of brain disease that is the ultimate origin of this struggle. Yet, as I noted before, there's currently no scientific "test"—like a blood test or a brain scan—showing reliable and reproducible patterns that is used to make a psychiatric diagnosis.

To be fair, even within general medicine there are diagnoses, such as migraine headache, whose ultimate cause(s) remain(s) elusive, yet we still accept the diagnosis—it's a real struggle!—and encourage treatment for it, knowing we need to do further study. Again, this is how medical science progresses. Peptic ulcer disease (ulcers in the stomach or first part of the intestine) is a great example of how an evolving understanding of causation has resulted in more targeted treatment. We now know that underlying many ulcers is an infection caused by the bacterium *Helicobacter pylori*. So now treatment consists not only of standard acid-reducing medications but also antibiotics to treat the infection. Yet it was helpful to have the descriptive category "peptic ulcer disease" and its associated standard treatment approaches even before the offending bacterial agent was discovered. Similarly, we should not be too quick to dismiss diagnostic categories as unhelpful simply because medical science has not explained why, for example, schizophrenia or bipolar disorder or social anxiety generally looks the way it does.

But what we see within psychiatry is a proliferation of diagnoses over time, as I noted earlier. A symptom-driven, descriptive approach fosters "splitting" rather than "lumping" diagnoses.[6] Having more diagnostic categories does not mean that we are "discovering" specific dysfunction at the brain level that led to those new classifications. But—and this is very important—ambiguity about causation doesn't mean that the struggling person isn't experiencing real suffering. He is. She is. But it *does* mean that we must be careful

---

6. A notable exception in the *DSM-5* is the folding of individual diagnoses such as Asperger's disorder, childhood disintegration disorder, and others into the broader diagnostic category of "autism spectrum disorder." Here is a clear example of scientific inquiry and observation modifying psychiatric classification.

about what we *assume* regarding the cause or causes of the person's struggle. Let's be honest about what we know and don't know. Let's not be reductionistic and assume that the biological piece is primary and ultimate in the diagnosis and treatment for all categories of psychiatric disorders. As noted earlier, the *DSM* does *not* claim to know the causes of each of the entities it describes.

In light of the *DSM's* honest admission of ignorance regarding the "whys" behind a particular struggle, you may be thinking, "Aren't you being overly critical of the secular classification system?" Interestingly, this critique of the psychiatric diagnostic system as overly descriptive and symptom-driven does not arise simply from our Christian understanding of human beings as those who not only suffer but also are active moral agents. In fact, spirited internal debates persist within psychiatry as to the nature and classification of mental illness. Thoughtful secular psychiatrists and psychologists continue to grapple with how to define and classify mental disorders. Listen to what Dr. Paul McHugh, the former chairman of psychiatry at Johns Hopkins, says:

> Because the manual [the *DSM*] fails to identify what underlies the symptomatic expression of a condition, it cannot suggest intelligible principles relating one disorder to another or illuminate why certain of them bunch together.[7]

If the profession of psychiatry is honestly wrestling with these fundamental questions, then we too can't ignore them.

To summarize, the most significant limitation of psychiatric diagnoses is that they describe human thought, emotion, or behavior but do not explain why the person has these experiences. This creates confusion and misunderstanding among the public, which perceives the system to be more definitive than it is. Now, more briefly, let me mention several additional concerns with the psychiatric diagnostic system.

---

7. Paul R. McHugh, "Striving for Coherence: Psychiatry's Efforts Over Classification" *JAMA* 293, no. 20, (2005): 25-26.

Chapter 5

PROBLEMS AND PITFALLS: ABNORMALIZING THE NORMAL

A second concern with the diagnostic system is that *psychiatric diagnoses have the potential to abnormalize the normal through over-diagnosis.* On the one hand, when the *DSM* diagnosis includes the criterion that the problem must cause "clinically significant distress or impairment," this should guard against over-diagnosis. On the other hand, the subjectivity of "clinically significant distress or impairment" and the proliferation of diagnostic categories mean that more people may be caught in a particular diagnostic net over time. You might call this the Psychiatric Field of Dreams: "If we can describe it, you can have it."[1] Dr. Allen Frances, who was the chair of the Task Force that created the *DSM-IV*, calls it "the medicalization of ordinary life."[2]

---

1. I'm riffing off the line, "If you build it, they will come" from *Field of Dreams* (Universal Pictures, 1989). The difference between over-diagnosis (making a positive diagnosis when it is not actually present, which leads to an increase in the observed frequency of the condition) and a true increase in the incidence of mental illness is complicated to discern statistically. For a helpful overview see Ronald W. Pies, "Is There Really an 'Epidemic' of Psychiatric Illness in the US?" *Psychiatric Times,* May 1, 2012, http//www.psychiatrictimes.com/print/159694.

2. Allen Frances, *Saving Normal: An Insider's Revolt Against Out-of-Control Psychiatric*

While his book has a sensationalistic tone in places, lacks scientific rigor to support certain assertions, and builds upon a thoroughly secular evolutionary worldview, Frances does raise important issues regarding the problem of over-diagnosis. His aim is to reform and rebalance psychiatry, not demean it as a profession: "Saving normal, as I use the term, is not meant to deny the value of psychiatric diagnosis and treatment. Rather it is an effort to keep psychiatry doing what it does well within its appropriate limits. It is equally dangerous at either extreme—to have either an expanding concept of mental disorder that eliminates normal or to have an expanding concept of normal that eliminates mental disorder."[3]

This is the irony (at least in America): Those with milder (and perhaps self-limited) forms of emotional distress are increasingly diagnosed as mentally ill, while those incapacitated with psychosis and other severe psychiatric problems remain under-diagnosed and under-treated, especially if they lack the financial resources and social connections to facilitate medical care. This latter reality reminds us that in our zeal to raise concerns about the diagnostic enterprise we must avoid an extreme that fails to recognize true deviance from the spectrum of normality even if it remains challenging to define the limits of "normal" (but a bit more on that later).

The problem of over-diagnosis is exacerbated by the fact that most mental health diagnosis and treatment is carried out by primary care physicians, who may or may not be skilled at using existing *DSM* diagnostic criteria. I remember years ago in medical practice trying to restrain the diagnostic enthusiasm of the medical residents I was supervising. Too often they were overzealous to diagnose all kinds of mental health issues on the basis of a short interview and diagnostic questionnaires. Screening questionnaires

---

Diagnosis, DSM-5, Big Pharma, and the Medicalization of Ordinary Life (New York: William Morrow, 2013). For a more thoroughly researched account of the proliferation of psychiatric disorders and over-diagnosis, see Horwitz, *Creating Mental Illness*. See also Allan V. Horwitz and Jerome C. Wakefield, *The Loss of Sadness: How Psychiatry Transformed Normal Sorrow into Depressive Disorder* (New York: Oxford University Press, 2007).

3. *Saving Normal*, 18-19.

can be a helpful first step in highlighting the existence of a problem, but more in-depth conversations are necessary to evaluate the nature of a person's struggle. It is not unusual for a psychiatrist to spend at least an hour for an initial evaluation with a patient. Primary care providers rarely have this extended time. But time-driven or insurance-driven factors must take a back seat to diagnose well.

Further, there is a symbiotic relationship between psychiatric diagnosis and the pharmaceutical industry, which is true for other branches of medicine as well. The presence of a drug that could potentially treat a problem may well increase the diagnosis of that problem, for better or for worse. Peter Kramer puts it this way: "We may mask the issue by defining less and less severe mood states as pathology, in effect saying, 'If it responds to an antidepressant, it's depression.' Already, it seems to me, psychiatric diagnosis had been subject to a sort of 'diagnostic bracket creep'—the expansion of categories to match the scope of relevant medications."[4] This problem is intensified by direct-to-consumer advertising by drug companies, which critics argue increases patient self-diagnosis and pressure on physicians to prescribe medications unnecessarily.[5]

In all this discussion about over-diagnosis, I want to be very careful. Putting someone in a diagnostic category who technically doesn't meet the criteria doesn't mean that the person isn't struggling! Diagnosis or not, we need to listen well to people's stories. Many counselees I meet with don't have a "diagnosis" but they rightly expect that I will listen to their problems with compassion, ask good questions, help them understand their struggles from a biblical perspective, and encourage them to take wise steps to address both suffering and sin in their lives.

One final comment here: Who determines what is "normal" or "abnormal" with regard to cognition, emotion, and behavior? A

---

4. *Listening to Prozac,* 15.
5. For a detailed analysis of this trend see Julie Donohue, "A History of Drug Advertising: The Evolving Roles of Consumers and Consumer Protection" *Milbank Quarterly* 84, no. 4 (2006): 659-699, doi:10.1111/j.1468-0009.2006.00464.x.

subset of physicians or psychologists? Society at large? Individuals? At the end of the day, "normal/abnormal" is not the only (or best) binary to categorize people because it doesn't, in and of itself, reference the reality that we are image bearers who stand before the living God as responsive and responsible people (Genesis 1:26-27; Romans 1; Colossians 3:10). A person without a diagnosed mental disorder ("normal" according to the *DSM*) may in fact be living a life oriented away from God (and thus "abnormal" as it relates to God's design for humanity). A person with a diagnosed mental disorder ("abnormal" according to the *DSM*) may in fact be living a life oriented toward God ("normal" as it relates to God's design for humanity). This leads to the next problem or limitation with the psychiatric diagnostic system.

Chapter 6

PROBLEMS AND PITFALLS: REDEFINING BEHAVIOR

A third concern with the psychiatric diagnostic system is that *some psychiatric diagnoses redefine behavior that Scripture would characterize primarily as sin.* That is, some psychiatric diagnoses "medicalize" sinful behavior. Over twenty years ago, an orthodontist in the Philadelphia suburbs was indicted for and pleaded guilty to fondling a teenage patient. He subsequently maintained that he was entitled to $5000/month disability from his insurance company since he was unable to continue his orthodontics practice due to a diagnosis of what the *DSM-5* now calls "Frotteuristic Disorder": "recurrent and intense sexual arousal from touching or rubbing against a nonconsenting person, as manifested by fantasies, urges, or behaviors [such as masturbation]."[1]

While this may be an extreme example, certain *DSM-5* diagnoses are fundamentally moral-legal issues recast as mental illness. To name a few, consider other disorderly sexual desires

---

1. http://articles.philly.com/1994-07-14/news/25845173_1_warren-graboyes-ortho dontist-sexual-disorder. Diagnostic criteria are found in the *DSM-5*, p. 691.

(labeled paraphilias), including voyeurism, exhibitionism, pedophilia, sadism, masochism, and more. Or consider the "disruptive, impulse-control, and conduct disorders," such as oppositional defiant disorder, conduct disorder, pyromania, kleptomania, or "intermittent explosive disorder" (recurrent verbal or physical aggression). In calling attention to these issues, I am not saying that people who manifest these struggles do not need skillful and compassionate help. They do! The redemption that Jesus offers indeed extends "far as the curse is found." They *need* wise biblical counseling. But we should take care that behaviors that are first and foremost violations of the first and second great commandments to love God and others (Matthew 22:34-40) are not neutralized, sanitized, or fully excused by a particular diagnosis. Their victims deserve at least that much.

On the other hand, the church too often has recast mental illness fundamentally as a moral (spiritual) issue, for example, equating psychosis with demon possession or viewing severe depression as a mere failure of the will. This approach of classifying suffering as sin is equally problematic.

In fact, a person's struggle can exist in both arenas of experience at once. Several years ago I read the story of a forty-year-old married schoolteacher who began to collect child pornography (in addition to his more long-standing habit of collecting adult pornography).[2] He also engaged the services of prostitutes, which he had never done before. When he began to make sexual advances toward his step-daughter, he was reported to the authorities and legally removed from the home. He was diagnosed with pedophilia and faced the choice of going to jail or successfully completing a twelve-step inpatient sexual addictions program. He chose the latter but soon after starting the program, he sought sexual favors

2. J. M. Burns and R. H. Swerdlow, "Right Orbitofrontal Tumor with Pedophilia Symptom and Constructional Apraxia Sign," *Archives of Neurology* 60, no. 3 (2003): 437-40.

from fellow program participants as well as staff members. He was dismissed from the program and ordered to report for jail time.

The night before his incarceration was to begin, he took himself to a local ER complaining of headaches and the fear that he would sexually assault his landlady. He was admitted to the psychiatric ward but after demonstrating a difficulty with walking, the neurology staff evaluated him. A MRI revealed a large frontal brain tumor. The mass was removed—and the man's sexual compulsiveness disappeared. In fact, following discharge he was able to successfully complete the twelve-step program. However, a number of months later he began once again to collect child pornography secretly. When this was discovered, a repeat brain MRI revealed regrowth of the tumor! The tumor was once again surgically removed—and the man's pedophilic desires faded.

Was his problem medical or spiritual? Yes! Was he a sufferer or a sinner? Yes! Was he a victim or a perpetrator? Yes! Of course, the overwhelming majority of pedophiles do not have a brain tumor associated with their deviant desires. This is an unusual case. No doubt the presence of the brain tumor directly correlated with *this* particular man's pedophilic desires. No doubt regular medical follow-up should be part of his total care. But even the secular authorities were not willing to overlook the moral-legal aspects of his struggle. He was accountable for his actions.

Chapter 7

PROBLEMS AND PITFALLS:
THE INFLUENCE OF CULTURE

A final concern is that *social-cultural values influence the inclusion or exclusion of specific diagnoses from the* DSM *and impact the prevalence of diagnosis.* As my friend and psychiatrist John Applegate has said, "The *DSM* is a cultural document. It *influences* society and itself is influenced *by* society."[1]

Consider two examples. The first is homosexuality, which was included in the *DSM-I* (1952) and *DSM-II* (1968) as a mental disorder. In the *DSM-III*, published in 1980, it was no longer included as a diagnosis. While I fully agree with this change in status—homosexuality is principally a moral-spiritual issue and not an expression of disease/disordered mental health[2]—the change came about for purely sociological, not scientific reasons. Sexuality researcher Alfred Kinsey surveyed a large population of men in the 1960s and found that around ten percent of men engaged in exclusively homosexual relationships. Kinsey concluded that any behavior

---

1. Talk given to CCEF counseling staff, May 14, 2013.
2. This is not to say that there aren't bodily or brain-based factors that may contribute to same-sex attraction, particularly for those who have experienced exclusive same-sex attraction from their earliest memory. Nor does this discount the mental anguish and persecution those struggling with same-sex attraction may endure.

engaged in by such a large percentage of the population should not be considered evidence of disease but rather represent normal variation. Kinsey's conclusions helped fuel a consensus decision by leading psychiatrists to remove homosexuality as a diagnosis.[3]

A second example is that of ADHD (Attention-Deficit Hyperactivity Disorder). I have no doubt that many children and adults do have relative brain differences or weaknesses that make selective attention, staying on task, and following a sequence of directions more difficult. There is much neuropsychological research that increasingly pinpoints various deficits in such abilities. This is a genuine struggle for some children and adults that goes beyond willful disobedience. Therefore we need to approach each person individually, weighing the pros and cons for both diagnosis and use of medication.

But the diagnosis and medical treatment of ADHD (in children at least) could not have proliferated to the extent it has in the last twenty years apart from a number of factors, including (1) an American society that esteems academic performance and success and continues to push these standards into the preschool years; (2) an often overloaded public school system where crowded classrooms and lack of funding often make it impossible to carry out the behavioral and structural interventions that would benefit these children; (3) full-scale pharmaceutical company promotionals for ADHD drugs; (4) screen-based media excess, which may contribute to the problem by promoting distraction, shifting attention, and instant gratification.[4]

There are also cross-cultural differences in diagnosis that underscore the sociological dimension. In an article entitled "Why French Kids Don't Have ADHD," psychologist Marilyn Wedge notes that while nine percent of American school-aged children

3. Laura D. Hirshbein, *American Melancholy: Constructions of Depression in the 20th Century* (New Brunswick: Rutgers University Press, 2009), 5.

4. See Nicholas Carr, *The Shallows: What the Internet Is Doing to Our Brains* (New York: W. W. Norton & Company, 2011).

have been diagnosed and are taking medication, only 0.5 percent of French children have been diagnosed, largely due to French psychiatrists viewing the behavioral problems as something to be addressed primarily with social and relational interventions.[5] The *DSM-5* maintains via population surveys that "ADHD occurs in most cultures in about 5% of children and about 2.5% of adults." It goes on to say, "Differences in ADHD prevalence rates across regions appear attributable mainly to different diagnostic and methodological practices. However, there also may be cultural variation in attitudes toward or interpretations of children's behaviors."[6]

To wrap up the last four chapters, the concerns with the diagnostic system when considered together suggest that psychiatric diagnoses have less functional authority than we might initially believe. The *DSM* may be the best secular classification scheme available, but it remains fraught with difficulties identified from within psychiatry itself. This leads to a number of ministry implications.

---

5. Marilyn Wedge, "Why French Kids Don't Have ADHD," www.psychologytoday.com/blog/suffer-the-children/201203/why-french-kids-don't-have-adhd.

6. *DSM-5*, 61-62. At the same time it is important to note that the disordered thoughts, emotions, and responses to external stressors characteristic of many *DSM*-designated mental illnesses are enduring transcultural phenomena that predate modern classification schemes. Some patterns of mental unrest are fairly stable across cultures, showing that such suffering is a universal problem. Nonetheless, we should recognize socio-cultural influence in the understanding and classification of many current psychiatric issues.

Chapter 8

IMPLICATIONS FOR MINISTRY

Hurting and struggling people will continue to receive these diagnoses. How should the limitations I just described impact the way you counsel such strugglers, particularly if you are in the "too warm" camp? I have identified four implications to keep in mind as you encounter these diagnoses in ministry.

The *first implication*, particularly if you lack clinical mental health training but desire to provide rich pastoral care and counsel, is this: "Don't be scared off by a diagnosis." The modern church, in general, has abdicated responsibility for the care of individuals with psychiatric diagnoses. Often this is due to fear on several levels. We fear difference. We fear what we don't understand. We fear not having what it takes to help—"What do I have to add to the care of this complex problem?" But don't let a diagnosis get in the way of seeing the whole person and providing a measure of needed help!

I knew a man in my former church who struggled with paranoid schizophrenia. Despite the use of multiple medications, he continued to have bouts where accusatory voices filled his head, telling him that he was worthless and that he ought to kill himself. What did he need most? Fine-tuning of his medications? Certainly that was something important to pursue, given the complexity of his psychoactive medical treatment. But I think what he especially needed at those times was a friend. A friend who would listen with compassion and patience. A friend who would take seriously the impact of those demeaning and frightening voices in his head. A friend to remind him of God's favor, care, and presence in his experience of isolation, confusion, and loneliness. A friend who would pray for him and read the Psalms with him. A friend who would highlight that, in Jesus, nothing could separate him from the love of the Father (Romans 8:38-39). A friend who expected both personal and corporate benefit from having this man as a part of the body (1 Corinthians 12:21-26). You can be that friend. I can be that friend. And that's apart from having any particular medical expertise with schizophrenia (which of course he needs as well). Don't let the diagnosis obscure the multiple ways in which you can draw near to the person before you.[1]

A *second implication* for both strugglers and helpers is that the diagnosis is not the struggler's identity. Even with clear-cut medical problems we don't say, "I am diabetes" or "I am cancer." Why would we say, "I am bipolar" or "I am ADHD" or "I am borderline," as though that is the sum total of our personhood? The temptation is for the diagnosis to be the sun around which all the rest of life orbits. But people are far more wonderfully complex than a diagnosis can capture!

The fact is that we're all somewhere on the spectrum represented by many of these symptom lists. So we should always look for the commonalities. Because psychiatric diagnoses are not discrete entities with radically sharp boundaries, we should be able to see at least a little bit of ourselves in this other person's experience. For the person with the diagnosis, it means that he or she is not so radically different from others, and that decreases a sense of isolation and stigma. (Later I'll talk about the need to recognize the differences and discontinuities in our experiences, not just the commonalities.)

---

1. For many helpful ministry suggestions that complement these ideas, see Edward T. Welch, "Ten Ways Ordinary People Can Help Those with Psychiatric Problems," *The Journal of Biblical Counseling* 28, no. 2 (2014): 22-38.

A related, *third implication* is that diagnosis is not destiny. If "God's image bearer," "Christ's servant," and "beloved son/daughter" are more primary and biblical ways of identifying strugglers, then it is important to keep in mind God's ultimate transforming agenda for all his people in the midst of their suffering and sin. Consider just of a few of the passages that stagger our imagination:

- "No eye has seen, nor ear heard, nor the heart of man imagined, what God has prepared for those who love him" (1 Corinthians 2:9).
- "So we do not lose heart. Though our outer self is wasting away, our inner self is being renewed day by day. For this light momentary affliction is preparing for us an eternal weight of glory beyond all comparison, as we look not to the things that are seen but to the things that are unseen. For the things that are seen are transient, but the things that are unseen are eternal" (2 Corinthians 4:16–18).
- "And I am sure of this, that he who began a good work in you will bring it to completion at the day of Jesus Christ" (Philippians 1:6).
- "Beloved, we are God's children now, and what we will be has not yet appeared; but we know that when he appears we shall be like him, because we shall see him as he is" (1 John 3:2).

There are no "exception clauses" here for any believer, and that is radically good news for anyone (helper or struggler) who might be tempted to view a diagnosis as a final word. God's way of describing believers and their destiny is profoundly humanizing even as we are reminded of our groaning this side of glory. One of my counselees recently said something very insightful in this regard: "Psychiatric labels don't tell a story." What she meant was that labels and diagnoses don't and can't give a full-orbed picture of a person's life and where God is at work.

This flows naturally into a *fourth implication*: A diagnosis, if present, is one of many starting points for ministry, and certainly not an *end* point. Rather than a destination, it is an invitation to a journey. The diagnostic category becomes an impetus to understand people's experiences as well as we can, using biblical categories. This includes an exploration of fears, desires, motivations, their relationship with God, their bodily strengths and weaknesses, their relationships with others, and the circumstances of their lives—the very places we would consider in helping someone even in the absence of a diagnosis.

In explaining human experience, the Bible highlights the primacy of our moral-spiritual disposition before God (i.e. the "heart"—see Luke 6:43-45 and Matthew 15:10-20) but also notes the importance of bodily weakness or strength, relational influences both good and bad, and situational or circumstantial pressures or blessings. Comprehensive ministry appreciates the relative contributions and interrelationships of all these aspects of human experience.[2] We want to understand people so well and do such a careful job of re-interpreting their struggles through a biblical lens that a diagnostic label serves only as shorthand for their experience rather than the sum total of their experience.[3]

We want to be watchful that the presence of a diagnosis doesn't give us tunnel vision that blinds us to other important aspects of the person's experience. As the psychotherapist Irvin Yalom notes, "Once we make a diagnosis, we tend to selectively inattend to aspects of the patient that do not fit into that particular diagnosis, and correspondingly overattend to subtle features that appear to confirm an initial diagnosis."[4]

---

2. For further details see Emlet, "Understanding the Influences on the Human Heart."

3. In this sense the relationship between psychiatric diagnoses and knowing the details of a person's life parallels the relationship between systematic theology and Scripture. Systematic theological categories are helpful summaries and shorthand formulations of Scripture, but no substitute for digging into the details of the Bible itself.

4. *The Gift of Therapy: An Open Letter to a New Generation of Therapists and Their Patients* (New York: Harper Perennial, 2009), 5.

So, going back to our person who meets the diagnostic criteria for social anxiety disorder, we seek to build relationship and understand his or her experience: "Tell me the specifics of your struggle. What situations prompt this anxiety? What factors have contributed to this struggle? What has helped? What hasn't helped? Where have you seen God at work in the midst of your difficulties? Where do you struggle to trust God? What's your worst-case scenario? When are you encouraged?"

Maybe you'll find out that he was a mildly anxious person who performed poorly at one point in time and was ridiculed for it. Or that he was a confident speaker who for inexplicable reasons suffered a panic attack during one of his talks and now avoids speaking altogether. Or that she grew up in a family where her parents were overprotective and fearful themselves. Maybe you'll find that the person is angry with God. Or that in the midst of overwhelming anxiety she runs to God. Or that he is a gourmet cook who enjoys blessing his family with fine food. Or that her favorite book is Anthony Doerr's *All the Light We Cannot See*. But you'll learn none of these things if you are content to stop with the diagnosis as the "hook" that basically explains the person. (Of course, a thoughtful secular psychiatrist will be attentive to many of these factors as well, albeit not the all-important spiritual categories.)

These details shape your overall ministry to the person. They reveal places of strength and growth to celebrate. They highlight significant and formative experiences that are worthy of lament and further biblically guided conversation. They show places where your friend needs to realign thoughts, attitudes, and actions with God's picture of wholeness in Scripture. The bottom line is that knowing the details keeps before you a real person in all his complexity. A person with hopes, fears, dreams, suffering, temptations, sin, joys, and sorrows—not so different from you after all.

In contrast to psychiatric classification (whether the older psychoanalytic or the newer categorical/descriptive), a biblical view of the person is full-orbed! Biblical categories expand our view of the struggling person and lead neither to hyper-spiritual nor hyper-physical ministry approaches. Long before psychiatric categories existed, wise pastors and shepherds took seriously the spiritual, physical, temperamental, relational, and situational factors of especially troubled individuals in their care and saw this approach as congruent with Scripture. Consider works such as Gregory the Great's *Book of Pastoral Rule* from the fifth century or Timothy Rodger's *Trouble of Mind and the Disease of Melancholy* from the Puritan era, which carefully, compassionately, and truthfully ministered to individuals in all their complexity.

Scripture is both richly descriptive *and* speaks to issues of cause. Biblical categories expand, not reduce, our understanding of people. As I get to know someone struggling with social anxiety, what biblical themes might emerge as I hear his story? While I can't do justice to a full-orbed approach, here are some ways I might walk with a struggler.

First, I would highlight where I see the Spirit already at work in the person's life. The apostle Paul does this at the beginning of most of his epistles. For example, in his letter to the Corinthians (a church with as many problems as people, it seemed!) he begins by affirming their standing and calling in Christ and pointing out the gifts God has given them (1 Corinthians 1:1-9). From that sure foundation he *then* tackles their issues and problems. Similarly, I want to be aware of what strengths, gifts, and fruit of the Spirit the social anxiety struggler brings to the table, so that we're able to build together on this foundation of God's good work. I want to highlight the person's identity in Christ (and all that he currently possesses by virtue of union with Jesus) when the temptation grows to escape the perceived scrutiny of others.

In someone who has been teased or bullied as a possible contributor to her social anxiety, I want to affirm that God hears the cry of the oppressed and that he holds oppressors responsible

(Psalm 9:9-10; Psalm 10; Jeremiah 23:1-4; Ezekiel 34). Jesus himself knows intimately the pain of ridicule and mistreatment (Isaiah 53; Mark 14:53-15:20) and invites us to draw near to him in our weakness (Hebrews 4:15-16; 1 Peter 5:7).

As to the experience of fear and anxiety—it's all over the pages of Scripture. In fact, the most common exhortation in the Bible is "do not be afraid." Generally, this does not sound like "WHAT'S WRONG WITH YOU ANYHOW?!" but more like a parent comforting a frightened child, "Don't worry . . . I'm here . . . don't be afraid." One goal I have for people struggling with social anxiety is to grow in calling out to God in the midst of their distress. At its core, anxiety is less situational and more relational: Is there really someone there for me or am I all alone? Does anyone care? I want to help people talk less to themselves and more to God as they press into their anxiety (Psalm 46:1; Isaiah 41:10).

The Bible also highlights that we are persons of moral agency who have motives driving our behaviors. Perfectionism, performance, people-pleasing, desires for success and recognition before others, avoidance of appearing weak (and more) may be part of the gasoline that's revving the engine of anxiety. It's important to address these underlying desires and fears with the hope and substance of the gospel. Our hearts are also exposed by suffering—those who are responding to this trial with anger and unbelief I want to direct back toward the Lord. Those who continue to cry out to God humbly I want to encourage in their perseverance even as we work together to improve their anxiety.

Finally, Scripture takes seriously that we live in bodies. I will pay attention to what physical symptoms of anxiety the person has—rapid heart rate, hyperventilation, light-headedness, tremors, and more. Overcoming anxiety is a whole-person endeavor. "Be still, and know that I am God" (Psalm 46:10a) involves learning to quiet both our minds and our bodies (see also Psalm 131).

I have taken some time to slow down and give just a taste of how Scripture speaks richly on multiple levels to the person struggling with social anxiety in order to guard against diagnostic tunnel vision. I spoke recently with a young man who told me that, while he was taking an overload of courses in college, working fifty hours a week, and sleeping just three hours a night, he sought medical help for increasing anxiety. After a short conversation his physician diagnosed him with "Generalized Anxiety Disorder" (a *DSM* category broader than social phobia) and gave him medication, which helped somewhat with the anxiety but caused a host of other problems. Finally, with the help of his pastor (and a wiser physician) he took stock of the pressures he faced, the choices he was making, and the desires and fears that drove those choices. He took better care of his body and his soul and was eventually able to wean off his medication. In this particular case the diagnostic shorthand "Generalized Anxiety Disorder" did not serve him well.

At the end of the day, we always want to submit psychiatric diagnosis to biblical diagnosis. We want biblical categories and themes to make sense of what we observe in others. Even then we need to remain humble, realizing that a complex array of factors we may not fully understand could contribute to the person's struggle. The diagnostic task, whether using biblical categories or secular ones, is never like following a simple recipe. Wisdom is key.

Now, you may be thinking, given all that I've written, "What help do psychiatric diagnoses provide anyhow? You've provided appropriate cautions that have kept me from becoming too warm toward the diagnostic system, but now I feel downright chilly toward this system of classifying people's struggles!" Again, I want us to have a wise and balanced assessment, so let's explore some of the benefits of psychiatric categorization as we minister to others.

Chapter 9

THE VALUE OF PSYCHIATRIC DIAGNOSES IN MINISTRY

There are ways that psychiatric diagnoses are useful at a macro-(medical-societal-cultural) level of care. They improve reliability in diagnosis among different mental health providers, are foundational in psychiatric research, guide insurance reimbursement, and serve as the basis for educational services, all of which are valuable. Just ask any parent of a child with special educational needs and you'll learn the importance of receiving a proper and explicit diagnosis.

But I want to focus on the potential usefulness of psychiatric classifications at the micro-level, in the context of one-another ministry. I hope this section will especially help those who are "too cold" toward these diagnostic categories.

First, psychiatric diagnoses organize suffering into categories that prompt focused attention. Put another way, the *DSM* helps you identify *patterns* of experience. It makes you aware of human struggles you perhaps didn't know existed and therefore encourages a caring and careful exploration of such struggles.

When I was a counseling intern at CCEF, one of my first counselees was a gentleman diagnosed with Asperger Syndrome. I had never heard of Asperger Syndrome before. By looking at the diagnostic criteria for Asperger's and learning that it was an autistic spectrum disorder, I was able to go into my early sessions with at least the basic contours of a typical struggle in mind. That, in turn, allowed me to ask well-suited questions that he could answer and flesh out with details of his experience. It helped me to better discern when my counselee might be *unable* to do something rather than simply *unwilling* to do something. It helped me to better distinguish between weakness and sin, between "can't" and "won't."

Now, if you are someone who is very skeptical of psychiatric diagnosis, you may say that I could have obtained the same information with good data-gathering skills. Perhaps, but I believe it would have taken longer. *And* I may not have seen the relationship between the parts of my counselee's experience. While we have seen the danger of putting all our eggs in the diagnosis basket, let's not overlook patterns of struggle that have been identified in the *DSM*.

One corollary of the idea that a diagnosis represents a clustering of experiences is this: we can profit from the published experience of those who work, perhaps exclusively, with one type of problem. In my work with counselees struggling with obsessions and compulsions, I have gained insight by reading both secular and Christian authors. In all cases, I submit what I'm reading to a biblical framework, since secular conceptualization of people's struggles and secular methodologies to help them are not "neutral." That is, they come with a particular slant on human beings and their problems that will not generally be in line with Scripture. At the same time, case observations from secular practitioners can send us back to Scripture to further understand and develop a biblical perspective of what they saw in incomplete ways.

For example, in my early work with people enslaved by obsessions and compulsions, I found it instructive to read about the six patterns of thinking commonly present in those diagnosed with OCD (obsessive-compulsive disorder): inflated responsibility, over-importance of thoughts (taking one's thoughts too seriously), overestimation of threat, the importance of controlling one's thoughts, intolerance of uncertainty, and perfectionism.[1] I might have identified those same patterns of thinking as I accumulated case wisdom, but having those patterns in mind early on gave me a jump start in considering how biblical themes and categories address the views of God and self that underlie those ways of thinking.

From a biblical perspective our cognition (our thought life) is not neutral. That is, our thinking is "covenantal"—either oriented toward revealed truth about God and his world or away from it. A persistent thought—"I must be absolutely sure I turned off the stove" (even after I've checked it five times already)—reveals the need for a growing trust in God's power and presence in the particulars of life. It reveals a mindset in which I am totally responsible for preventing catastrophe in my life. It reveals the need to entrust ultimate care for my life to a loving Father in that moment of indecision and fear. The non-neutrality of cognition is also evident (and perhaps more easily demonstrated) in the catastrophic, black-and-white thinking often present in depression: "I'm a total failure." Or "Nobody likes me." These statements carry an interpretation of life that has become unmoored from the realities of redemption the person possesses in Christ.

Second, diagnoses remind us that this person's experience is indeed different from mine. This keeps us from oversimplifying and suggesting well-meaning but potentially superficial approaches to a person's struggle. (Of course, I highlighted the flip side of this

---

1. David A. Clark, *Cognitive-Behavior Therapy for OCD* (New York: The Guilford Press, 2003), 112.

earlier: overreliance on a diagnosis may also lead to well-meaning but superficial approaches to the person's struggle.) Now, hopefully, we would come to similar conclusions just by sitting with the person and proactively entering his or her world. Diagnosis or not, we want to take the time to know someone before we dive into perceived solutions for the problem. But the presence of a diagnosis may mean that while there *are* commonalities of struggle between us, this person is likely to be struggling in more specific and intense ways. For example, we all get anxious, but not all of us have experienced panic attacks. We all have seasons of discouragement but not all of us have months of bone-numbing depression. We all have experienced scary events but not all of us are haunted by flashbacks and intense fear. Many of us like order in our lives but far fewer of us are paralyzed with the need to have perfect symmetry and organization in every part of our living space. These differences cannot be overlooked.

Why? The greater the intensity of suffering, the greater the need to carefully study people and carefully study the Scriptures in order to bring wise biblical perspective to their problems. A diagnosis sometimes sends us running back to the drawing board in terms of how we seek to use the biblical story to minister to someone. It's easier to minister to someone very similar to us. It's more difficult with someone different from us. A diagnosis waves a yellow caution flag that says, "Slow down! Be quick to listen and slow to speak! Take the time to discern the complexity of this person's struggle as a sufferer and sinner before God."

Third, certain diagnoses suggest particular patterns of severity and danger. If you don't see a symptom within a larger context in which certain thought processes, emotional fluctuations, and actions hang together, you run the risk of minimizing potential danger. For example, is the excessive energy, talkativeness, and self-focus you've seen in your friend over the last two months a manifestation of pride and self-centeredness? Possibly. But have you considered that those symptoms might represent the early stages of mania? If that's true, it suggests that an even higher level of vigilance is needed, both spiritually and medically.

Fourth, along these same lines, *some diagnoses remind us of a more central role of the body in a person's struggle.* Psychiatric diagnoses remind us that we are embodied souls. We *know* this clearly from Scripture! But functionally speaking, we sometimes over-spiritualize troubles with emotions and thoughts. When you consider the spectrum of psychiatric diagnoses, it is clear that years of research demonstrate that some diagnoses may have a stronger genetic (inherited) component of causation than others. These include schizophrenia, bipolar disorder, autistic spectrum disorder, and perhaps more severe and recalcitrant forms of depression (melancholia), anxiety, and OCD.[2]

Another way of saying this is that although psychiatric diagnoses are descriptions and not full-fledged explanations, it doesn't mean that a given diagnosis or symptom holds no explanatory clues at all. Not all psychiatric diagnoses should be viewed equally. Some *do* indeed have long-standing recognition in medical and psychiatric history, occur transculturally, and therefore are not merely modern, Western "creations" that highlight patterns of deviant or sinful behavior, as critics would say. Observations that have held up among various observers across time and place suggest that some people may have greater bodily "risk" to develop certain patterns of disordered thinking, mood, and behavior.

For example, I'm going to approach psychosis differently than social anxiety, although I will take seriously the struggle in both cases. I'm especially going to take seriously the ministry priority of medical treatments (e.g. the use of antipsychotics) for the person with psychosis. Still, in both cases I'm going to look for the many factors that together may contribute to the person's struggle. And

2. https://www.nih.gov/news-events/nih-research-matters/common-genetic-factors-found-5-mental-disorders.

I'm always going to look for how biblical truth and an ever-present God full of grace and mercy connect with this pattern of struggle.

It is an oversimplification to suggest that unless we can see structural changes at the level of the brain or isolate the singular cause (as with an infectious disease such as strep throat), a diagnosis is not "valid." There is no doubt that the *DSM* represents a spectrum—and some diagnoses are more socio-culturally driven than others, as I mentioned earlier. But other diagnoses do have quantifiable, consistently observed brain-based pathology, which underlie descriptive signs and symptoms (such as the dementias or narcolepsy). *Most* diagnoses in the *DSM* (what normally comes to mind when you think of a psychiatric disorder) reflect a blend of various potential causative factors including inherited biological predisposition, situations and experiences, effect of significant relationships, exposure to toxins in the environment, patterns of thinking and desire, personal choices and learned responses, and orientation toward or against God, to name a few prominent ones.[3] And within a given diagnostic category (depression or OCD for example), certain contributing factors may be more prominent than others. At the end of the day, the goal is not simply to confirm or condemn a given diagnosis but to carefully, persistently, lovingly, and biblically bring God's redemption to bear upon people who struggle with the problems encapsulated in a diagnostic description.

---

3. And it becomes even more complex when you realize that all these various factors are involved in a complex feedback relationship involving the human brain.

Chapter 10

CONCLUSION: WHAT'S IN A NAME?

What's in a name? How should we think about psychiatric diagnoses? It's clear that psychiatric diagnoses are descriptions, not explanations. This should create a ministry mindset of careful inquiry. We want to expand secular categories of understanding people, not be constrained by them. Diagnoses are a starting point, not an ending point for ministry. They do not confer identity, nor do they provide a full understanding of people. At the same time, there are a number of benefits of the psychiatric diagnostic system that underscore the need to take certain patterns of suffering and sin seriously if we are to care for people wisely.

The bottom line is to know the person in front of you as well as you possibly can. Hippocrates's adage remains true for us today: "It is more important to know what sort of person has a disease than to know what sort of disease a person has."[1] Both proponents and skeptics of psychiatric classification should agree on one thing: we are wonderfully and distressingly complex creatures. This should

---

1. Quoted in Frances, 26.

humble us and promote dependence on God as we seek to understand and provide help within a biblical framework to those who are especially troubled.

If you came to this portion of the book tending toward one extreme or the other in your attitude regarding psychiatric diagnoses, I hope you have been challenged to move forward with a ministry approach that is neither too hot nor too cold, but just right. May God give us wisdom to strike that balance as we minister holistically to others with biblical fidelity.

Part 2:
Understanding
Psychoactive Medications

INTRODUCTION: WHAT DO YOU HEAR?

In Part 1 of this book, I attempted to present a balanced assessment
of psychiatric diagnosis. In Part 2, I want to do the same regarding
psychoactive medications. I'll start with several actual case studies
that illustrate some of the questions we need to wrestle with as we
seek to discern a biblical perspective on psychiatric medications.

~ ~

You have been working for six months with a member of your
congregation who struggles with serious depression and anxiety.
After walking alongside her in her suffering, you have together
identified ways in which her perfectionism and her mistrust in
the goodness and mercy of the Lord contribute to her anxiety and
depression. She is slowly making progress. You see her more consistently using the Psalms to move toward God to voice her fears
and disappointments. She is less hypercritical of herself and others.
Then, over a one-month period, you see remarkable change. It's
as if she's coming out of hibernation. She shakes off her sluggish

spirituality before your eyes. The Word comes alive to her in new and fresh ways. She has a growing excitement to serve others. Her depression and anxiety lessen week by week. You rejoice! And then she tells you that four weeks earlier, she saw her primary physician who prescribed Prozac, which she has been taking since.

So, how do you view her change now? Are you disappointed? Thankful? Confused? Do you change your counseling approach? Should you be more proactive in recommending an evaluation for medication, particularly for those counselees who seem "stuck" or are making slow progress? Do you prayerfully consider going to medical school so that you, too, can prescribe Prozac?!

~ ~

Another person comes to you for help with long-standing obsessions and compulsions. He has been on six different medication combinations in the past, none of which have significantly helped him. He is discouraged about his lack of progress and about the twenty-pound weight gain and frequent headaches he has experienced over the last six months on his latest medical regimen. Where do you begin?

~ ~

A member of your congregation tells you that he is taking Tegretol, Zoloft, and Abilify for a diagnosis of bipolar disorder. He is interested in coming off these medications and wants your advice before he returns to his psychiatrist. More specifically, he has developed the conviction that he should, with God's help, be able to live medication-free. How should you proceed? What information would you want to know? Should a life characterized by robust faith and repentance make medication *un*necessary?

~ ~

These vignettes show that familiarity with psychoactive medications is a must for pastors, counselors, and other helpers in the church. We live in a time when more and more problems in living are attributed to brain-based dysfunction. Medication is touted as an important (if not the *most* important) aspect of treatment within the psychiatric community. In popular street-level understanding, it is often *the* treatment of choice.

As I noted earlier, Christians remain divided on this issue. Some would say that medication is usually appropriate, viewing it as a God-given tool to relieve mental suffering. Others are more cautious, recommending medication only in more severe situations. Still others decry the use of psychoactive medication as a "cop-out," arguing that a basic posture of gospel-centered obedience is all that is really necessary.

As Christians, we can't just "listen to Prozac."[1] We need a biblically-based philosophy to guide the use or non-use of medications. We need to know not only the "what" and "how" of psychoactive medication use, but also the "why" or "why not." And we need strategies. How should we proceed in difficult cases like those mentioned above?

To that end, I have several specific goals in this section of the book: (1) to familiarize you with the basic classes of psychoactive medications; (2) to review what we know about the mechanism of action and efficacy of such drugs with a particular focus on antidepressants; and (3) to discuss a biblical approach to psychoactive medications.

---

1. See Peter D. Kramer, *Listening to Prozac* (New York: Penguin Books, 1993).

Chapter 11

CLASSES OF PSYCHOACTIVE MEDICATIONS

The term "psychoactive" medication refers to those chemical substances that are designed to enter the brain tissue from the bloodstream to cause changes in mood, thoughts, emotions, and behavior. The adjectives "psychotropic" or "psychiatric" are synonyms for psychoactive. These terms can be used interchangeably. In fact, most any medication, at high enough doses, can have psychoactive (side) effects. (For example, a certain high blood pressure pill may cause drowsiness or impaired ability to concentrate.) But my focus is on those classes of medications *designed* to have effects on the brain.[1] I will summarize the various classes now. See Table 1 for an overview.

---

1. A helpful, fairly comprehensive (and compact) resource is John Preston's "Quick Reference Guide to Psychotropic Medication," found at www.PsyD-fx.com.

Category of Drug	Used to Treat	Examples of Available Drugs
Antidepressants	Depression	Tofranil, Elavil, Prozac, Zoloft, Paxil, Celexa, Wellbutrin, Effexor, Remeron, Cymbalta
Mood Stabilizers	Bipolar Disorder	Lithium, Tegretol, Depakote, Lamictal
Antiobsessionals	Obsessive-Compulsive Disorder	Anafranil, Zoloft
Psychostimulants	Attention Deficit Hyperactivity Disorder (ADHD)	Ritalin, Concerta, Focalin, Dexedrine, Adderall
Antipsychotics	Schizophrenia, psychosis, hallucinations, delusions	Thorazine, Mellaril, Haldol, Risperdal, Zyprexa, Geodon, Abilify
Anxiolytics	Anxiety	Valium, Librium, Klonopin, Ativan, Xanax, Zoloft, Paxil
Hypnotics	Insomnia	Ambien, Sonata, Lunesta

Table 1. Classes of Psychoactive Medications

Antidepressants are probably the class of medications we are most familiar with. Early antidepressants, developed in the 1950s and '60s, such as Tofranil (imipramine) and Elavil (amitriptyline), are still used today, but have been overshadowed by the "SSRIs"—selective serotonin reuptake inhibitors—such as Prozac (fluoxetine), Zoloft (sertraline), Paxil (paroxetine), and Celexa (citalopram), which were released starting in the late 1980s. Other antidepressants with varied chemical compositions include Wellbutrin (buproprion), Effexor (venalafaxine), Remeron (mirtazapine), and Cymbalta (duloxetine). Three relatively new agents include

Fetzima (levomilnacipran), Viibryd (vilazodone), and Trintellix (vortioxetine). No one subclass of antidepressants has proved consistently more effective than another and newer antidepressants are not more effective than older ones, although they do tend to have less sedative side effects than the older antidepressants.

At the same time, there are subtle differences between various antidepressants that factor into a psychiatrist's choices when prescribing such medications. For example, Prozac tends to be more "activating" than Paxil, which has more sedative effects, although they are both part of the SSRI class. Someone whose depression is associated with more agitation and anxiety might be prescribed Paxil over Prozac, though both are associated with the reduction of depressive symptoms.

Mood Stabilizers are used to treat bipolar disorder. These are also called "anti-mania drugs." Lithium, discovered in 1949, has been the gold standard within psychiatry for many years, although it can be associated with potentially dangerous side effects. More recently, medications that initially were used for seizure disorders were observed to have a mood-leveling effect. These include Tegretol (carbamazepine), Depakote (divalproex) and Lamictal (lamotrigine), to name a few.

Antiobsessionals are medications used to treat obsessions and compulsions. Many of these are the SSRIs I noted earlier, along with Anafranil (clomipramine). Notice that many medications, particularly the SSRIs, have multiple potential uses authorized by the Food and Drug Administration (FDA). Right away that tells you that these medications are less like "smart bombs" that work with laser precision, and more like conventional bombs with widespread effect on systems of neurotransmitters in the brain. This lack of specificity reminds us just how little we understand the neurobiological component in psychiatric problems. I'll speak more about this later.

Psychostimulants have been used since the 1950s to treat the symptoms of Attention-Deficit Hyperactivity Disorder (ADHD). These include Ritalin (methylphenidate), Concerta (the sustained release version of methylphenidate), Focalin (dexmethylphenidate), Dexedrine (dextroamphetamine), and Adderall (mixed amphetamines). Because they are stimulants, they have the potential for abuse if not used as prescribed.

Antipsychotics are used to treat the symptoms of psychosis, including the hallucinations and delusions characteristic of schizophrenia. The older antipsychotics, used since the 1950s, include Thorazine (chlorpromazine), Mellaril (thioridazine), and Haldol (haloperidol). Due to very severe side effects, some of which are permanent, these drugs were limited in their use.

However, the creation of a new generation of antipsychotics has led to more patients being treated, particularly bipolar patients whose mania may or may not have features of psychosis. These newer antipsychotics, which are essentially equal in efficacy to the first generation antipsychotics, include Risperdal (risperidone), Zyprexa (olanzapine), Geodon (ziprasidone), and Abilify (aripiprazole). The newest antipsychotics include Invega (paliperidone), Fanapt (iloperidone), Latuda (lurasidone), Saphris (asenapine), Rexulti (brexpiprazole), Nuplazid (pimavanserin), and Vraylar (cariprazine).

Early research suggested that the second-generation antipsychotics had fewer side effects. More recent research suggests the potential for equally serious but different kinds of side effects when compared to the first-generation antipsychotics.[2]

Anxiolytics (anti-anxiety medications) are used to treat the symptoms of anxiety. Historically, physicians have used a subclass known as benzodiazepines for treating anxiety and panic. These included drugs such as Valium (diazepam) and Librium

2. See J. A. Lieberman, et al., "Effectiveness of Antipsychotic drugs in Patients with Chronic Schizophrenia," *New England Journal of Medicine,* 353, No. 12 (2005):1209-23.

(chlordiazepoxide), and more recently, Klonopin (clonazepam), Ativan (lorazepam), and Xanax (alprazolam).

The problem with the benzodiazepines, when used regularly and over the long term, is the potential for tolerance, dependence, and withdrawal. Tolerance means that your body requires more of the drug over time to get the same effect. Dependence is your body saying it needs a certain level of the drug to feel normal and to prevent withdrawal. Withdrawal symptoms, including increased anxiety, rapid heart rate, sweating, and more occur when the drug is stopped abruptly due to this physical dependence. In some cases (for example, from Xanax) this withdrawal can be life-threatening. In general, physicians now use benzodiazepines for the short-term treatment of anxiety, and are more likely to prescribe the SSRI class (e.g., Zoloft, Paxil) for longer-term treatment.

Hypnotics are prescribed for insomnia. Older medications were in the benzodiazepine class but now physicians choose newer drugs, such as Ambien (zolpidem), Sonata (zaleplon), Lunesta (eszopiclone), and others that have less addictive potential.

Although I mentioned some specific concerns above, it is important to note that side effects are common with each of these classes of psychoactive medications. Drowsiness and weight gain are very common. Sexual side effects, such as decreased libido and the inability to experience orgasm, may be as high as sixty percent in the SSRI subclass. As we will see later, the potential benefits of using medication might outweigh the costs, including side effects. So simply note at this point that these are not benign agents. They may help, but they can also harm—hence their regulation by the FDA!

Chapter 12

DO MEDICATIONS TREAT
A "CHEMICAL IMBALANCE"?

Now that I have familiarized you with the basic categories of psychoactive medications, let's tackle the question, "How do they work?" Are they treating "chemical imbalances"? This is certainly the lay understanding, as fueled by biologically-oriented psychiatry and pharmacological marketing. But do psychoactive drugs correct imbalances in body chemistry?

To answer that question, I need to give you a crash course in basic neuro-anatomy. Don't worry, I'll try to make it painless! In the brain there are billions of nerve cells (neurons) that communicate with each other via chemical substances called neurotransmitters. In simple terms, the sending cell releases neurotransmitters into the space between it and the receiving cell. The receiving cell has receptors for the neurotransmitter and is activated when the neurotransmitter binds to it. Following activation, the neurotransmitter is released from the receptor site. Then it either: (1) is taken back up into the sending cell to be repackaged and used again, (2) remains in the space between the neurons, or (3) gets destroyed.

Scientists have discovered over 200 neurotransmitters. Some that you may be familiar with are serotonin, dopamine, and norepinephrine. The theory is that psychiatric problems result from an imbalance in, or a dysregulation of, neurotransmitters or neurotransmitter systems in certain parts of the brain. For example, some conclude that depression results from a deficiency of serotonin, so treatment involves using psychoactive medications to address this deficiency. The impact of these treatments is often vividly portrayed in pharmaceutical ads in before and after schematics of the patients' brains. But what do we really know?

First, since we are unable to measure neurotransmitter levels in the brain of a person being treated with these medications, we cannot definitively prove that these drugs are responsible for any changes in the person's symptoms. Note that this is very different from other medical diagnoses. For example, for hypothyroidism we can directly measure a low amount of thyroid hormone, or for diabetes we can directly measure a high amount of glucose in the bloodstream of a particular patient. Treatment of both conditions will lead to direct changes in blood measurements. But because we cannot measure neurotransmitters, we cannot draw the same kinds of conclusions about the impact of the psychoactive medication on a particular person's symptoms.

Second, we do not know exactly how these medications work in humans. What we do know is how these medications work in test tubes with animal brain tissue; this research is then extrapolated to humans. This, in and of itself, is appropriate for testing hypotheses, but it cannot tell you what is actually going on in the human brain. Listen to what even a very biomedically-oriented scientist, pharmacologist Stephen Stahl, has to say:

> In general, contemporary knowledge of CNS [Central Nervous System] disorders is in fact largely predicated on knowing how drugs act on disease symptoms, and then inferring pathophysiology [i.e., what's wrong physically in the brain] by knowing how the drugs act. Thus, pathophysiology is *inferred*

rather than proved [emphasis mine], since we do not yet know the primary enzyme, receptor, or genetic deficiency in any given psychiatric . . . disorder.[1]

Here is an example from the description of a specific drug. The *PDR (Physician's Desk Reference)* describes Zoloft (sertraline) this way: "The mechanism of action of sertraline is *presumed* [emphasis mine] to be linked to its inhibition of CNS neuronal uptake of serotonin."[2] In other words, Zoloft *may* impact the neurotransmitter serotonin in the human brain as it does in basic laboratory research, but we're not certain. Nor are we exactly sure how this might translate to an antidepressant effect, particularly in light of the complex interaction of various neurotransmitter systems within the human brain.

This is important. If neuroscientific and psychiatric researchers acknowledge the current limitations of biomedical hypotheses regarding the origin of psychiatric symptoms, how much more should we, as those who bring biblical counsel, acknowledge the complex nature of these struggles, taking into account underlying spiritual, biological, relational, situational, and societal-cultural factors![3]

---

1. Stephen M. Stahl, *Essential Psychopharmacology: Neuroscientific Basis and Practical Applications,* 2nd ed. (Cambridge: Cambridge University Press, 2000), 104. Although this was written over fifteen years ago, it remains essentially true . . . and at the same time, simplistic in its own right. Why? Because it is unlikely that there will ever be *one primary* neurophysiological mechanism discovered for a given psychiatric diagnostic entity. One current exception may be the experimental intranasal use of Orexin-A for the *DSM* diagnosis "narcolepsy," which directly treats a deficiency of orexin (hypocretin) in the brain. See Alberto K. De la Herrán-Anita, et al. "Narcolepsy and Orexins: An Example of Progress in Sleep Research," *Frontiers in Neurology,* April 18, 2011. https://doi.org/10.3389/fneur.2011.00026. See also Chittaranjan Andrade and N. Sanjay Kumar Rao, "How Anti-depressant Drugs Act: A Primer on Neuroplasticity as the Eventual Mediator of Antidepressant Efficacy," *Indian Journal of Psychiatry* 52, no. 4 (2010): 378-386. http://www.indianjpsychiatry.org/text.asp?2010/52/4/378/74318.

2. *Physician's Desk Reference,* 59th edition (Montvale: Thomson PDR, 2005), 2681.

3. As we saw in Part 1, the ongoing disagreement within psychiatry itself regarding how to understand and classify mental disorders shows the insufficiency of a purely biological orientation to the cause and treatment of psychiatric symptoms.

So, at best we can say that these drugs modulate, or change, neurotransmission in some way, and that seems to be associated with symptom reduction in a statistically significant proportion of those tested in clinical drug trials. But are these drugs treating a chemical imbalance in the human brain? We don't really know—maybe. We know that they seem to alleviate symptoms in some people but do not know exactly how. More helpful than a simplistic notion of "chemical imbalance" is to say that these medications are likely involved with changes in neural networking and neurotransmission in the brain—but this remains unproven at this time. Our knowledge is incomplete. However, by pointing out that the actual knowledge about how these drugs work in the brain is limited, I'm not saying we should avoid such medications. I'm saying that if we do use them, we should be aware of what we really know. We have much to learn and a cautious optimism is in order, not an unbridled and uncritical enthusiasm.

Chapter 13

HOW EFFECTIVE ARE PSYCHOACTIVE MEDICATIONS?

Space does not permit me to analyze each class of psychoactive medications, so let me focus primarily on the use of antidepressants, since it is the class you will encounter the most frequently in one-another ministry. First, remember that a drug cannot come to market in the United States unless the Food and Drug Administration (FDA) approves it, based upon the results of clinical drug trials. More specifically, a study medication has to beat a placebo (a chemically inactive substance or treatment) by a statistically significant margin to be considered effective.

So, how well do antidepressants work? Compared to placebo, they have been shown in published studies to help in mild, moderate, and severe depression.[1] Keep in mind that it is not unusual

---

1. A meta-analysis (combining the results) of individual studies showed that "the magnitude of benefit of antidepressant medication compared with placebo increases with severity of depression symptoms and may be minimal or nonexistent, on average in patients with mild or moderate symptoms. For patients with very severe depression, the benefit of medication over placebo is substantial." Jay C. Fournier, Robert J. DeRubeis, and Steven D. Hollon, "Antidepressant Drug Effects and Depression Severity: A Patient-Level Meta-analysis" *JAMA* 303, no. 1 (2010): 47-53. (Of note, there are pros and cons to drawing conclusions from meta-analyses compared to the original individual studies but it's beyond the scope of this resource to address that topic.)

for 35 percent or more of patients receiving a placebo to respond favorably. This shows the power of belief: If I *think* a treatment I'm receiving may be effective (whether it is or is not), it is more likely to have that effect. The higher the placebo effect, the more the actual, active drug must demonstrate its effectiveness in order to be considered superior to the placebo.[2]

Take, for example, a clinical drug trial of 200 depressed patients, 100 of whom receive a new antidepressant and 100 of whom receive a placebo. The standard protocol for such studies is "double blind"— neither the patients nor the researchers know who has the active medication and who has the placebo, so as not to bias the results.[3] Let's say 35 percent of the placebo group responds favorably, with a reduction of their depression (this is the placebo effect) and 70 percent of the active drug group responds favorably (see Figure 1).

---

2. Technically, the placebo effect is not just related to expectation/belief, but to all of those factors, tangible and intangible, which may be having a therapeutic effect that is not related to the active ingredient.

3. If I *know* I am getting a placebo—an inactive substitute—I will be less likely to respond favorably to it; the placebo effect declines. If I know I am getting the active drug, it is more likely to work; that is, the placebo effect (even for the active drug) is boosted. "Blinding" the study participants seeks to avoid this bias. Of course, if I experience side effects because I am on the active drug, I may conclude that I am taking the study medication, which also biases in favor of the drug.

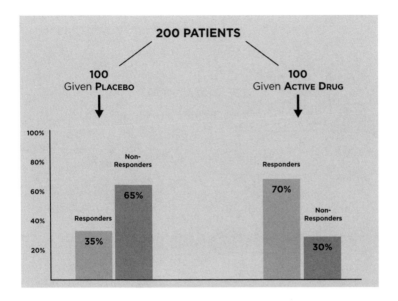

Figure 1.

Looks good, right? But remember that part of that 70 percent could be the power of belief (a placebo effect of the active drug) and another part could be the actual biochemical effects of the drug itself. So, at the end of the day, of those 100 patients who got the active drug, 30 percent did not respond, 35 percent may have responded by virtue of a standard placebo effect, and 35 percent may have responded due to the actual effects of the drug itself (see Figure 2).[4]

4. Some, like Irving Kirsch, argue that most, if not all, of the favorable response to the drug is an enhanced or boosted placebo effect. (See Kirsch, *The Emperor's New Drugs: Exploding the Antidepressant Myth* [New York: Basic Books, 2010]). For a rebuttal, see Peter Kramer, *Ordinarily Well: The Case for Antidepressants* (New York: Farrar, Straus, and Giroux, 2016). Also see Frederic M. Quitkin, et al., "Validity of Clinical Trials of Antidepressants," *American Journal of Psychiatry* 157, no. 3 (2000): 327-337.

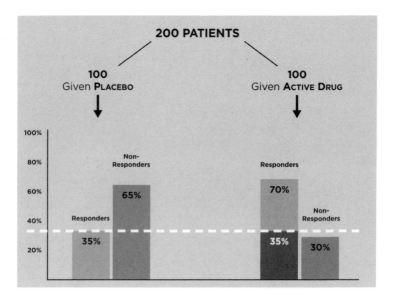

Figure 2.

We should conclude that overall there seems to be a modest drug effect, but it's certainly not a "chemical cure" (although for that 35 percent such efficacy may be critical, even life-saving, depending on the severity of the depression). It is important to remember that these clinical studies ultimately say nothing about how an *individual* person will or will not respond when given an antidepressant. At this point there is no definitive way to predict who will respond best to which treatment, although there are some available biomarker tests that may help guide physicians as to which class or dose of medication may be more effective in certain patients, particularly in cases when they haven't responded to other treatments.[5]

5. There is debate about just how effective these laboratory tests are in guiding care. For a more cautious approach see J. de Leon, "The Future (or Lack of Future) of Personalized Prescription in Psychiatry" *Pharmacological Research* 59, no. 2 (2009): 81-89, doi: 10.1016/j.phrs.2008.10.002.

We can also ask if medications are more effective than counseling for depression. This is tricky to answer because there are many types of psychotherapy in practice. One cannot speak of "counseling" in general when considering the available research. It's important to know what type of psychotherapy is used in the particular research study. Cognitive or cognitive-behavioral therapy (CBT) is the most frequently studied method of counseling.

Individual studies have revealed that even in moderate to severe depression, cognitive therapy was as effective as medication at four months of treatment, although medication might bring more rapid improvement compared with psychotherapy. Note that the degree of the psychotherapy's effectiveness may well depend on the counselor's experience and expertise.[6] There is also evidence that cognitive therapy is superior to medication in preventing relapse once medication and/or counseling is discontinued.[7] Other studies seem to show that the combination of psychotherapy and medication may be superior to psychotherapy or medication alone.[8]

What does this research mean for helpers who are committed to providing pastoral care and biblical counsel to those struggling with depression? At the very least the research reminds us that forms of care other than medication have been shown to be effective for those who are depressed. Specifically, methods of care that involve listening, questioning, reasoning, dialogue, evaluating

---

6. R. J. DeRubeis, et al., "Cognitive Therapy Vs. Medications in the Treatment of Moderate to Severe Depression," *Archives of General Psychiatry* 62 (2005): 409-416.

7. S. D. Hollon, et al., "Prevention of Relapse Following Cognitive Therapy Versus Medication in Moderate to Severe Depression," *Archives of General Psychiatry* 62 (2005): 417-422. See also Robert J. DeRubeis, Greg J. Siegle, and Steven D. Hollon, "Cognitive Therapy Versus Medications for Depression: Treatment Outcomes and Neural Mechanisms," *Nature Reviews Neuroscience* 10 (2008): 788-796, doi: 10.1038/nrn2345.

8. S. M. De Maat, et al, "Relative Efficacy of Psychotherapy and Combined Therapy in the Treatment of Depression: A Meta-analysis" *European Psychiatry* 22, no. 1 (2007): 1-8; Pim Cuijpers et al, "Adding Psychotherapy to an Antidepressant in Depression and Anxiety Disorders: A Meta-analysis" *World Psychiatry* 13, no. 1 (2014): 56-67, doi: 10.1002/wps.20089.

thoughts, and changing behaviors are helpful in depression. This should not surprise those of us who have a biblical framework for understanding people; these activities are part of the warp and woof of day-to-day intentional Christian living before God in community with other believers. But the secular research does not "validate" biblical counseling compared to medication, nor do we need it to (although I am not opposed to empirical research). I offer these research conclusions simply to demonstrate that even secular research doesn't promote a superiority of medication in the treatment of all severities of depression.

It is important to remember that not all psychiatric symptoms respond equally well to psychotherapy and to medications. I have been highlighting treatment for depression, which itself shows great variety in symptoms and severity. Other problems, such as the psychotic symptoms of schizophrenia or the mania of bipolar disorder, generally require the use of medications for initial stabilization and long-term management. You can't ordinarily talk someone out of his delusions and hallucinations.

However, a multifaceted approach that includes counseling and other social interventions is still in order once the psychosis has been stabilized with medication. There is evidence that those with psychosis who receive CBT in addition to their medication have less distress and less functional deficits even if (for example) their auditory hallucinations have not fully resolved (presumably because their interpretations of those voices have changed).[9] Further, a recent study showed that people with a first episode of psychosis consistent with schizophrenia fared better (improved symptoms, more consistent employment or attendance at school,

---

9. Lucy Maddox, "What is CBT for Psychosis Anyway?" *The Guardian* Tuesday May 20, 2014, https://www.theguardian.com/science/sifting-the-evidence/2014/may/20/cbt-psychosis-cognitive-behavioural-therapy-voices?CMP=share_btn_link. See also E. Kuipers, et al., "London-East Anglia Randomised Controlled Trial of Cognitive-Behavioural Therapy for Psychosis. I: Effects of the Treatment Phase" *British Journal of Psychiatry* 171, no. 4 (1997): 319-327.

higher quality relationships) when they were receiving regular counseling (specifically, "resilience-focused individual therapy") and active family support (along with the standard medications) than when they were not receiving interventions beyond the usual medications and standard case management.[10] This should not surprise us as Christians, since we know that God designed us to live in a community of intentional, meaningful relationships.

So, what should we conclude from all this information, particularly with regard to antidepressants? They do seem to work—that is, improve mood and other symptoms of depression—in some people, some of the time, but they certainly are not the "silver bullet" that some make them out to be. Even if we conclude that medications are or might be effective for a particular person, they comprise only a part of the total approach to the person. Secular research shows the critical importance and efficacy of psychotherapy as well, as I noted. Further, as believers we hope not only for symptom reduction but also for tangible growth in love for God and love for people. Improved mood may correlate with these things, but not necessarily!

Medications may well change neurotransmission in the human brain at microscopic levels; they certainly are associated with change in the pattern of brain activity at "macroscopic" levels on "live action" brain scans such as positron emission tomography (PET scans) and functional MRIs (fMRIs). But then secular forms of counseling such as cognitive behavioral therapy have proven similarly effective in changing brain patterns.[11] In that sense, both medication and various forms of counseling work biologically—medication directly so, and counseling indirectly so.[12]

---

10. John M. Kane, et al., "Comprehensive Versus Usual Community Care for First Episode Psychosis: 2-Year Outcomes from the NIMH RAISE Early Treatment Program," *American Journal of Psychiatry* 173, no. 4, (2016):362-372.

11. DeRubeis, et al., "Cognitive Therapy Versus Medications for Depression," 788-796.

12. For a lay-oriented secular understanding see Louis Cozolino, *Why Therapy Works: Using Our Minds to Change Our Brains* (New York: W. W. Norton & Company, 2016).

As I noted earlier, my purpose here is not to scientifically prove the value of pastoral/biblical counseling by comparing it to the effectiveness of various psychotherapies.[13] Rather, my aim is simply to get you thinking about the fact that helping a struggling person to evaluate his emotions and thoughts and to bring them into line with reality affects change in depression. God does not bypass the body in the sanctification process. To the extent that a person's thoughts, emotions, desires, motivations, and actions align with God's revealed way of living in Scripture, our neural patterns should reveal that reality.

---

13. The relationship between secular psychological theory/practice and the Christian faith is a complex one. Helpful resources include David Powlison, *Seeing with New Eyes: Counseling and the Human Condition Through the Lens of Scripture* (Phillipsburg, NJ: P & R, 2003) and Eric L. Johnson, ed. *Psychology & Christianity: Five Views* (Downers Grove, IL: InterVarsity Press, 2010).

Chapter 14

WALKING THE WISDOM TIGHTROPE

We have assessed the biomedical data on the use of medications, but how should we assess the use of medications from a more explicitly biblical perspective? It is important to remember that we exist as body-spirit creatures. We are simultaneously body and soul. There's never a time we're not spiritually engaged. And there's never a time we are not bodily engaged. This means that attention to both physical and spiritual aspects of our personhood is mandatory in ministry. It is profoundly dehumanizing to ignore the "heart"—our moral-spiritual disposition and the responsibilities that go with it; and it is profoundly dehumanizing to ignore the body and the strengths and weaknesses that go with it.

What biblical-theological truths provide guidance? I *could* look at the places in Scripture where attention to the body is explicitly mentioned as a focus of "treatment": those passages include 1 Kings 19 (where God prescribed sleep, food, and water for Elijah) and 1 Timothy 5:23 (where Paul urged Timothy to take some wine for his stomach ailment). However, it is my assumption that the doctrines of creation, incarnation, and resurrection (among others) demonstrate the critical value God places upon our bodies. Therefore, my starting presupposition is that the body is an appropriate "target" for ministry, just as our moral-spiritual disposition clearly is. So my focus will lie on other aspects of biblical truth that inform the use or non-use of medications for the Christian.

Let me discuss some things I keep in mind as I consider the use of medications. You might call this "walking the wisdom tightrope" because you will see that a biblical approach balances different ministry priorities.

Walking the wisdom tightrope is not unique to this issue. The need for wisdom is characteristic of the way we live out our Christian faith each day. Consider the contrast between Proverbs 26:4 and Proverbs 26:5, which both describe how to handle a foolish person: "Answer not a fool according to his folly, lest you be like him yourself" (26:4); "Answer a fool according to his folly, lest he be wise in his own eyes" (26:5). Here are back-to-back verses that describe different ways of approaching a foolish person! Do I answer or do I not answer a fool? It depends! Both are appropriate biblical responses but, depending on the person and the situation (and the state of my own heart!), I may choose to live out verse 4 or I may choose to live out verse 5 in that moment.[1]

You will see a similar weighing of various factors as we look at biblical perspectives that help us assess the use or non-use of medications. Should we use medications or not? Spoiler alert—it depends!

---

1. I believe I first heard this insight during my biblical poetry class at Westminster Theological Seminary in the late 1990s, taught by Peter Enns.

Chapter 15

RELIEVING AND REDEEMING SUFFERING

Main idea: *It is a kingdom agenda to relieve our suffering and it is a kingdom agenda to redeem us (transform us) through suffering.*
When the kingdom comes in Jesus Christ, you see God's heart with regard to suffering in two ways. First, it is God's design to relieve the suffering that arose as a result of the fall. Consider how Mark 1 describes the activities of Jesus's ministry: teaching, exorcisms, healing those with various diseases, prayer, and cleansing a leper. Peter put it this way to Cornelius:

> God anointed Jesus of Nazareth with the Holy Spirit and with power. He went about doing good and healing all who were oppressed by the devil, for God was with him. (Acts 10:38)

Clearly a mark of the in-breaking kingdom is the relief of suffering. As the Christmas hymn "Joy to the World" reminds us, Jesus "comes to make his blessings known far as the curse is found." Relief of suffering is a good and necessary thing. This in fact is where history is going; in the new heavens and earth there will be no crying or pain (Revelation 21:4). So when we seek to bring relief from suffering now, we are keeping in step with God's plan of redemption. As the Puritan Jeremiah Burroughs said, contentment is "not opposed to all lawful seeking for help in different circumstances, nor endeavoring simply to be delivered out of present afflictions by the use of lawful means."[1] I believe medications can certainly be one of those lawful means. There is nothing inherently wrong with seeking relief from present suffering.

Still, you see a second strand of teaching in the New Testament: God's design to redeem the experience of suffering for believers because of their union with Jesus, the Suffering Servant. Paul calls this "participation in [Jesus's] sufferings" (Philippians 3:10, NIV). By virtue of our being in Christ, God is at work in the midst of our suffering, conforming us to the image of Christ. This is the very gateway to experiencing his resurrection power and glory. This is such an important New Testament perspective that I want to slow down and mention several passages in which this teaching is central:

> [T]hat I may know him and the power of his resurrection, and may share his sufferings, becoming like him in his death, that by any means possible I may attain the resurrection from the dead. (Philippians 3:10-11)

> The Spirit himself bears witness with our spirit that we are children of God, and if children, then heirs—heirs of God and fellow heirs with Christ, provided we suffer with him in order that we may also be glorified with him. (Romans 8:16-17)

---

1. Jeremiah Burroughs, *The Rare Jewel of Christian Contentment* (Carlisle: The Banner of Truth Trust, 1964), 22.

Beloved, do not be surprised at the fiery trial when it comes upon you to test you, as though something strange were happening to you. But rejoice insofar as you share Christ's sufferings, that you may also rejoice and be glad when his glory is revealed. (1 Peter 4:12-13)

Now I rejoice in my sufferings for your sake, and in my flesh I am filling up what is lacking in Christ's afflictions for the sake of his body, that is, the church. (Colossians 1:24)

For we do not want you to be unaware, brothers, of the affliction we experienced in Asia. For we were so utterly burdened beyond our strength that we despaired of life itself. Indeed, we felt that we had received the sentence of death. But that was to make us rely not on ourselves but on God who raises the dead. (2 Corinthians 1:8-9)

But he said to me, "My grace is sufficient for you, for my power is made perfect in weakness." Therefore I will boast all the more gladly of my weaknesses, so that the power of Christ may rest upon me. For the sake of Christ, then, I am content with weaknesses, insults, hardships, persecutions, and calamities. For when I am weak, then I am strong. (2 Corinthians 12:9-10)[2]

Former seminary professor Richard B. Gaffin, Jr., sums up these passages this way:

It is so natural for us to associate suffering only with the delay of Christ's second coming and to view suffering only in the light of what we do not yet have in Christ; but when this

---

2. Other passages include Romans 8:16-25, 2 Corinthians 4, James 1:2-4.

happens, we have lost sight of the critical fact that in the New Testament, Christian suffering is always seen within the context of the coming of the kingdom of God in power and as a manifestation of the resurrection life of Jesus.[3]

In other words, God is at work redemptively in the midst of our sufferings by virtue of our being united with the One whose suffering ultimately led to resurrection and glory.

So, while relieving suffering is a kingdom priority, seeking mere relief without a vision for God's transforming agenda in the midst of suffering may short-circuit all that God wants to do in the person's life. Another way of saying this is that we should be glad for symptom relief but simultaneously look for the variegated fruit of the Spirit: perseverance in the midst of suffering, deeper trust in the Father's love, more settled hope, love for fellow strugglers, gratitude, and more.

---

3. Richard B. Gaffin, Jr., "The Usefulness of the Cross," *Westminster Theological Journal* 41, no. 2 (1979): 229-246.

Chapter 16

HAZARDS TO SPIRITUAL GROWTH

ain idea: Too much suffering can be "hazardous" to spiritual growth and too little suffering may be "hazardous" to spiritual growth.

This is related to my first point. What do I mean here? Simply this: It is hard to find the "sweet spot" for spiritual growth. In the midst of intense suffering, whether it stems from the body or from other sources (relational strife, difficult life circumstances), there often is a greater temptation to become fearful, angry, and embittered. This was true of the Israelites in the wilderness. They had experienced the redeeming power of God in bringing them out of captivity. But despite God's provision they succumbed to the temptation to doubt his goodness in the midst of wilderness hardships. Or consider the response of Job's wife to Job in the midst of their suffering, "Curse God and die" (Job 2:9). Extreme suffering provokes our hearts to fear and anger. As we've seen, it's not a bad thing to seek deliverance from intense suffering and this can be done in a godly way, unlike the Israelites and Job's wife. For example, many psalms provide a model of crying out to God with integrity and humility in the midst of troubles and grief (Psalms 10, 22, 44, 73, 77, and 88, to name a few).

At the same time, a lack of suffering may bring the temptation to simply forget that "'in him we live and move and have our being'" (Acts 17:28). Temptation toward complacency and self-reliance can certainly happen when life is relatively easy. This was part of the problem God's people experienced once they left the wilderness and entered the Promised Land. Their dependence on him waned in the midst of material blessing (Deuteronomy 8:10-14; Judges 2:10-12). You see that same pattern in David (2 Samuel 12:7-9) and Solomon (1 Kings 10-11).

We are prone to wander from God when life is hard and when life is easy. Perhaps this is why the writer of Proverbs prays, "Give me neither poverty nor riches; feed me with the food that is needful for me, lest I be full and deny you and say, 'Who is the LORD?' or lest I be poor and steal and profane the name of my God" (Proverbs 30:8-9).

Here's another way of saying this: God-centered contentment is elusive in want *or* in plenty. Neither situation is the "ideal" for spiritual growth in a fallen world. Paul highlights this in Philippians 4:11-13 (NIV). He learned "the secret of being content in any and every situation, whether well fed or hungry, whether living in plenty or in want." He looked to the strength of Christ in all situations.

What does this mean with regard to the use or non-use of medications? Don't be too quick to cast off suffering as though immediate relief from trials is the only good God is up to. And don't think it's more "spiritual" to refrain from taking medications, as though character refinement through suffering is the only good God is up to. We don't choose our suffering in some masochistic way. Yet we *are* called to a life of walking in the footsteps of our suffering Savior. Christ teaches us a cross-centered and dependent lifestyle (Luke 9:23). And this is true in all situations of life.

Chapter 17

GIFTS OR GODS?

Main idea: *Medications are gifts of God's grace and medications can be used idolatrously.*

I believe it is right to view the development of psychoactive medications as a good gift from God, an extension of the ruling and stewarding function he gave to humanity at creation (Genesis 1:26-28). At its best, scientific discovery explores God's world in all its astounding complexity and seeks to alleviate some of the misery we experience as fallen creatures in a fallen world. As such, we should receive medications gratefully and humbly, but not forgetting the One who has given the necessary gifting and wisdom to scientists and physicians to discover such remedies. Ultimately he alone upholds all things with his righteous right hand (Isaiah 41:10).

Sadly, however, I have met people who are better evangelists for Prozac than they are for the living God. Rather than viewing medication as simply one component of a full-orbed God-centered body-soul treatment approach, they view it almost as if it was their salvation. By definition, this is idolatry: attributing ultimate power and help to something other than our triune God. If a counselee believes that what *ultimately* matters is fine-tuning the dose of his Paxil, and finds discussion of spiritual things superfluous or irrelevant, that's a problem.

How a person responds when the medication works—or doesn't work—reveals her basic posture before God. Thanksgiving and a more fervent seeking after God in the wake of medication success say one thing; a lack of gratitude and a comfort-driven forgetfulness of God say another. A commitment to trust God's faithfulness and goodness in the wake of medication failure says one thing; a bitter, complaining distrust of his ways says another.

So, receive the gift but look principally to the Giver. Whether a medication "works" or not, *he* is always working on your behalf.

Chapter 18

MOTIVES GOOD AND BAD

*M**ain idea: A person can have wrong motives for wanting to take medication and a person can have wrong motives for not wanting to take medication.*

Often, the most important issue in the use of medications is the attitude of the person to whom you are ministering. It's not that psychoactive medications in themselves are *either* "good" or "bad." Rather, it's how a person views and handles this potential treatment that makes the difference. I've had counselees who want a referral for medication immediately without really wanting to examine their desires, fears, thoughts, choices, and lifestyle. And I've had counselees who resist the recommendation to consider the use of medications for self-oriented reasons. Let me elaborate on these two scenarios.

What are problematic reasons for wanting to take medication? The first is a demand for immediate relief coupled with doubt about the benefits of looking at potential underlying issues. I remember meeting once with a young man with a recent history of anxiety associated with public speaking. Some of the things he said pointed to underlying tendencies toward people pleasing and a fear of failure—much to work with from a gospel perspective! But he was not interested in counseling. He was not interested in a gospel perspective on his struggle. Rather, he had made an appointment for the sole purpose of obtaining my recommendation for a provider who could prescribe an anti-anxiety medication.

A second questionable motive for wanting to take medication involves caving in to the pressures of others. Family and friends may push for medications due to their own discomfort in seeing the suffering of their loved one. Sometimes the pressure reflects a selfish desire to have their loved one back to normal so that life would be easier for *them*.

But there also exist problematic reasons for *not* wanting to take medication. Resistance to medication can be an issue of pride and self-sufficiency: "I should be strong enough without medication." Or the more spiritualized version: "I should be able, by trusting God more, to do this without medication." Another reason could be fear of disapproval and judgment by others: "What would people think?" Yet another concern is shame: "There's something seriously wrong with me if I have to take this medication."

Despite some who struggle with these aberrant motives, many people sincerely want to grow in Christ in the midst of their mental suffering and simply wonder about the pros and cons of medication. Many rightfully wonder about the potential side effects of using medication. These thoughtful persons remain open to starting—or not starting—medication, which is a wise posture before the Lord.

One final note: Unless you have a license to prescribe medications you will not be recommending *per se* that someone take (or not take) medications. The decision to start a medication should be made in consultation with a trusted physician. It is appropriate for a pastor or counselor to suggest such a consultation or assessment (although many people have already seen their physician by the time they see a counselor). I'll speak about this further in the "Putting It All Together" chapter to follow.

Chapter 19

MEDICATIONS AND THE HEART, FOR BETTER AND FOR WORSE

Main idea: Using medications may make it more difficult to address moral-spiritual issues and not using medications may make it more difficult to address moral-spiritual issues.

Scripture treats us as unified beings, having both spiritual and bodily aspects.[1] Given that we are fully integrated, body and spirit (heart) creatures, it is not surprising that bodily strength or weakness impacts us spiritually and vice versa, but I'll focus here on the impact of our bodily constitution on our spiritual lives.

Here's a simple example. Let's say that for various reasons outside your control you have had poor sleep for the last week. You're exhausted; you find it difficult to concentrate. You also find that you are more prone to grumbling and impatience. You see life through a grey lens. And then you get two great nights of sleep in a row. Suddenly, your world is sunnier. You have a new vitality, both physically and spiritually. Patience and kindness

---

1. For an extensive treatment of biblical anthropology, see John Cooper, *Body, Soul, and Life Everlasting: Biblical Anthropology and the Monism-Dualism Debate* (Grand Rapids: Eerdmans, 2000). For a briefer summary, see Welch, *Blame it on the Brain?* and Emlet, "Understanding the Influences on the Human Heart."

require far less effort. What just happened? A physical "treatment"—sleep!—impacted your spiritual life. The heart issues of grumbling and irritation have become less prominent. That's not necessarily a bad thing; we *are* called to be wise stewards of our bodies. Getting a good night's sleep is important. But in a time of "plenty" (sleep-wise), we shouldn't forget our sinful tendencies toward anger and complaining that were revealed in our weakness. Being tired does not give us license to treat others poorly. At the same time, we don't "invite" greater bodily stress so as to provoke and test our own hearts, as if we arrange the conditions for optimal spiritual growth. This is our *Father's* business, "mingling toil with peace and rest."[2] Once again, we don't *choose* suffering as though pain in and of itself is noble.

How does this relate to the use of psychotropic medications? Improving someone's symptoms (of anxiety, for example) doesn't necessarily address the underlying fears and desires that may be present. Might one feel better? Yes. Again, this may not be a bad thing in itself—remember Jeremiah Burroughs's earlier comment about seeking relief. But does the person retain the zeal to address the spiritual struggles underlying the anxiety now that those tendencies are less visible in day-to-day life? If perfectionism, a quest for material success, and a dread of failure underlie your anxiety in a new job, are you willing to tackle those bent desires first and foremost? And is there a commitment to address the situational factors that contribute to the experience of anxiety? For example, if your anxiety is associated with unrealistic demands at work, are you willing to address this situation with your boss? In my experience, more mature believers do indeed remember what they saw in the mirror and continue to take their soul to task in thought, word, and deed (James 1:23-25) even if they do use medication. They do recognize the importance of assessing and changing

---

2. Carolina Sandell Berg, "Day by Day and with Each Passing Moment," Hymn #676, *Trinity Hymnal* (Atlanta: Great Commission Publications, 1990).

contextual factors, on or off medication. But I have also had people who, after improvement in their symptoms with medication use, assume that no further work is required.

Conversely, there are situations, albeit more extreme, when a failure to use medication may make it more difficult to address a person's spiritual life. I counseled a young woman in a demanding graduate program who presented with insomnia, depression, severe anxiety, and suicidal thoughts. While her suicidal thoughts rapidly waned by simply airing them with me and another friend, her other struggles did not. She could affirm intellectually the promises of God, but it was like her soul was coated in Teflon; the truths of Scripture seemed to slide right off. While this disconnect is true for all of us to some degree, it seemed particularly prominent for her.

After several meetings, I saw how much her ongoing exhaustion from the insomnia was part of a vicious cycle. On the one hand, you could say that her insomnia, which was anxiety-driven, was a fruit of her fear and unbelief; as such, it should be the primary target of ministry. On the other hand, you could say that her bodily exhaustion was making it much more difficult for her to respond in a faith-filled way. *Both* are appropriate avenues for ministry. In the end, I thought that seeing a physician for a short-term course of sleeping medication might be beneficial to break the negative cycle she was in. In fact, that was the case. As she slept better, it wasn't as if her problems magically melted away; she still struggled with anxiety. But she was able to internalize spiritual realities and truly begin to engage with God, addressing issues of perfectionism, legalism, and fear of man, which were root causes of her anxiety and despair.

Think of it this way: Using medication in select situations may be analogous to calming the surface waters to allow for deep-sea exploration. You can't have a diving expedition if there is a gale on the surface of the water. Situations in which such "calming" might be helpful include (but are not necessarily limited to) the hallucinations and delusions of psychosis (whether associated with schizophrenia or mania) and severe or unremitting anxiety or depression, particularly if associated with suicidal thoughts and plans. These extreme cases are more clear-cut in their need for additional wise medical input. But we live in a culture that doesn't tolerate *any* hint of "rough seas" but yearns for the comfort of glassy calm waters. (I know that's *my* temptation!) This contributes to the overuse of psychoactive medication in some who only want a quick fix; they don't really want to taste the fruit that comes from persevering through choppy waters.

Can taking a medication actually assist in sanctification? Yes, in the same way that adequate sleep can assist in sanctification! It's not that you can buy holiness in a pill, but using medication in certain situations *may* help bodily conditions that allow for a greater spiritual flourishing.

Chapter 20

PUTTING IT ALL TOGETHER

What have we seen? The scientific witness is mixed. While psychoactive medications may help a certain percentage of individuals, the benefits do not rise to the level touted by pharmaceutical companies and popular opinion. In addition, these medications can be associated with significant side effects. Biblically we have seen that gospel-centered ministry targets both the bodily and moral-spiritual aspects of life, and that both relief of suffering and perseverance in the midst of suffering are consistent with God's design. We also noted the interdependence of body and spirit. Given these scientific and biblical perspectives, what should our practice in counseling and interpersonal ministry be with regard to psychoactive medications?

I hope you have seen that there is not a clear-cut "right" or "wrong" answer. There is no universal "rule" that we can apply to all people at all times. There is no simple algorithm. Rather, the use of these medications is a *wisdom* issue, to be addressed individually with those we counsel. There will always be a mix of pros and cons, costs and benefits to carefully consider. We must ask, "What seems wisest for this particular person with these particular struggles at this particular time?" Most often, addressing the person's suffering takes place without the use of medication. Yet, in some cases, after asking that question, we will lean toward more directly addressing potential bodily causes and correlates of the person's struggle by recommending an evaluation to consider the use of medication. Notice how I phrase that—"recommending an evaluation to consider . . . ." I'm not mandating. I'm not making a definitive recommendation. I'm simply suggesting an evaluation to consider if medication should be a part of the holistic approach to the struggle. Such an evaluation might also uncover primary medical problems masquerading as psychological disorders. For example, in someone with new-onset anxiety (especially if not clearly tied to situational factors), a physician would likely check thyroid levels since an overactive thyroid can be associated with physiological symptoms consistent with anxiety. In that case, primary and specific treatment for the thyroid condition is warranted, not an anti-anxiety medication.[1]

I'm most likely to recommend a medical evaluation when any of the following occur:

- symptoms are severe and unremitting,
- symptoms are not abating despite the person's engagement with the counseling process, or
- there is a high risk of suicide.[2]

---

1. For multiple examples of how medical problems can be associated with mental disorder symptoms see James Morrison, *When Psychological Problems Mask Medical Disorders: A Guide for Psychotherapists,* 2nd ed. (New York: Guilford Press, 2015).

2. Suicide assessment is a learned skill and should involve the input of wise and seasoned counselors. The goal with a seriously suicidal person is to ensure safety and stabilization, which may require emergency psychiatric consultation and hospitalization. For further details see Aaron Sironi and Michael R. Emlet, "Evaluating a Person with Suicidal Desires" *The Journal of Biblical Counseling* 20, no. 2 (2012): 33-41. See also S. C. Shea, *The Practical Art of Suicide Assessment: A Guide for Mental Health Professionals and Substance Abuse Counselors* (Hoboken, NJ: John Wiley & Sons, 2002).

I encourage you to develop a relationship with a trusted and wise psychiatrist who shares your strong biblical convictions and can provide consultation for these kinds of decisions. Such a person may or may not exist in your locale. Well-trained, clinically-savvy psychiatrists whose practice is governed by a robust biblical worldview are indeed few and far between! A family physician or internist with extensive experience in the use of psychoactive medications may be another option. The point is that pastors and biblical counselors (and wise secular counselors also!) don't make these decisions on their own; close communication with medical providers is essential.

Often enough, people come to me already on medications; the choice to start or not start them is a non-issue. This is generally because their primary care physician has prescribed such a medication, but they may have already seen a psychiatrist as well. Remember that the majority of psychoactive medications—particularly antidepressants—are prescribed by primary care physicians. But usually, even on medication, struggling people have realized that psychotropic drugs do not solve all their problems. They still need help to reconcile conflict, or to walk in faith not fear, or to address any of the multitudes of other problems that bring people to counseling. There's plenty to discuss apart from talking about the utility or non-utility of their medication. Whether on medications or off, the goal is always to help a person grow in love for God and for neighbor.

Let me illustrate with an orthopedic analogy. I liken the use of medications to the use of crutches, and I don't mean that in a pejorative sense. A person can experience many different injuries to the legs that don't require a set of crutches. He may have visible pain; he may have a limp initially, but the problem is self-limited with forms of treatment other than the support of crutches. Here I might think of milder experiences of depression, anxiety, and

OCD, for example, where medication (like the crutches) might not be needed.

Others require crutches to assist them after experiencing a more significant injury or surgery. They use them for a season while their bodies recover. Here I might envision a fairly severe postpartum depression or severe panic attacks treated by a briefer course of medication. Still others have a more significant disability and may need to use crutches for an extended time or perhaps for life, if the disability is permanent. Here I think of problems such as schizophrenia and bipolar disorder, where the disordered brain is having a stronger influence on the expression of mental health than other contributing factors, and therefore long-term use of medication seems warranted.

Then, there are times when someone may be relying too much on his crutches and it actually impedes progress. I experienced this as a teenager when I broke my ankle. After the cast was removed I was told to bear weight "as tolerated." But I didn't tolerate it very well! I continued to use my crutches for an extended time because putting weight on my ankle caused pain. At my follow-up visit, my orthopedist told me to throw away the crutches and learn to bear weight, despite the pain. It was hard work, but I learned again to walk without the aid of crutches. The bottom line is that all musculoskeletal problems are different and it takes wisdom to know when the additional support of crutches is necessary and, if so, for how long. The same is true of psychoactive medication.

The analogy is imperfect, of course. It's easier to determine if someone can walk unaided or not. It's far more challenging to assess what a person can or can't do in the midst of emotional suffering. We will always struggle to find a wise balance between attention to the spiritual and physical aspects of our personhood. Sometimes in retrospect we'll conclude that we should have recommended the possibility of medications earlier. Other times we will decide that we jumped the gun and that medication wasn't the wisest choice after all. But we can be sure that whether medication is part of the total ministry approach or not, God sovereignly acts, and "is able to do far more abundantly than all that we ask or think, according to the power at work within us" (Ephesians 3:20). He *will* accomplish the redemption that he has begun in us.

Chapter 21

THE WISDOM FRAMEWORK
IN ACTION

To conclude, let's return to the examples at the beginning of Part 2 and see how this "wisdom framework" might look in action. What about the woman experiencing depression and anxiety? Certainly we should rejoice in the remarkable changes in her life! But can we say *why* she has changed? No doubt the Prozac could be having brain-based biochemical effects that have fostered her spiritual growth, given the mysterious interface of body and spirit. Or she could be experiencing a placebo effect from the Prozac. Or the Prozac isn't really doing much, but God has himself intervened in his providential timing in a new and deeper way. At the end of the day, I remain unsure about the ultimate cause. But my goals would be the same for her: rooting her security in Christ's righteousness in a way that pushes against her perfectionism, turning to God as an ever-present help in the midst of anxiety, and moving outward in love toward others. I wouldn't make a huge issue of the medication right now, although I might inquire about her decision to see her primary physician. Did she feel that progress was too slow? Did family or friends urge her to go? What is *her* understanding about the value of the Prozac?

At some point in the future, if her spiritual growth is sustained and her depression and anxiety remain at bay, I would suggest talking with her physician about the possibility of discontinuing her medication. Most psychiatrists recommend taking an antidepressant for nine to twelve months before possibly stopping it. This assumes that the depression is not recurrent; if it were, a longer course may be considered.

It's not that the ultimate goal is being off medication—conformity to the image of Jesus Christ *is*! "Faith expressing itself through love" (Galatians 5:6, NIV) is the goal, whether you are on medications or not. But there's no indication at this point, by virtue of the severity or length of her struggle that she would need to be on medication long-term. In fact, the progress (albeit slow) she was making prior to taking the medication bolsters that hope.

The second person is experiencing the reality that medication is not a panacea for his obsessions and compulsions. For him, not only has medication not helped, its side effects have hurt him. While I'm dubious about the benefit of continuing his medical regimen, I would not recommend that he discontinue the medication(s) on his own. Instead, I would suggest that he speak with his physician about suspending the medication temporarily to see how he fares. If I were concerned about the quality and experience of his treating physician, I might recommend a consultation with a trusted psychiatrist. But apart from any decisions about medication, there is much work to be done in addressing his obsessions and compulsions from a gospel-centered framework.

Lastly, how would I approach the man who has the bipolar diagnosis and wants to discontinue his medications? I want to get a better idea about the nature of his struggle over time. When was he diagnosed? How severe were his symptoms? Did he have psychotic features? Has he had recurrences either on medication or off medication in the past? How compliant has he been with his medications? Has he ever been hospitalized? The more severe and recurrent his problem—and here I might get input from his family and friends—the greater the concern I would have about discontinuing medication. Ideally I would seek his permission to speak with his psychiatrist so that the approach could be as collaborative as possible. I would not want him to discontinue medications without the supervision of his prescribing physician.

In addition, I want to understand why he believes that God wants him to be medication-free. How has he come to that decision? Through a process of settled, prayerful dependence and the input of others who know him well? Or has his decision been impulsive and highly emotional? (A new onset of "super-spirituality" may in fact be a warning sign of mania.) If the man chooses to discontinue his medications, he will need close monitoring and follow-up. I would want to work closely with his psychiatrist, as well as members of his family and church community.

Let me conclude this portion of the book with a few brief reflections. We are body-spirit creatures. We should not be surprised that a physical treatment such as medication may be associated with symptomatic and perhaps more substantial change in people's lives. Medication can be an appropriate and even necessary part of someone's care, depending on the specific nature of a person's struggle.

Yet we must admit that a great deal of mystery remains about how psychoactive medications actually work in the human brain. We take care to remain balanced in our assessment of the effectiveness of medications. We neither exalt them nor disregard them. Even if we do view medication as a potential piece in a comprehensive ministry approach, we always seek to bring the riches of Christ's redemption to bear upon people's lives. Sinners will always need mercy, grace, forgiveness, and supernatural power to love God and neighbor. Sufferers will always need comfort, hope, and the will to persevere. Ultimately, *these* blessings are found not in a pill bottle . . . but in the person of Jesus Christ.

Chapter 22

GOLDILOCKS REVISITED

As you finish this book, take stock of your responses. Where did you resonate? Where did you want to push back? I have no illusions that you are in agreement with everything I've said. Mental health issues are very complex and this resource addresses only a portion of what is needed for a full-orbed practical theology of mental health and illness. But my hope is that if you began with a more extreme "hot" or "cold" posture regarding psychiatric diagnoses or medications, you have moderated somewhat (or at least are more open to doing so). If you began with a wiser moderate posture, aware of both the limitations and benefits of using psychiatric labels and medications for those with mental suffering, I trust that you now have a more robust biomedical and biblical rationale as you carry out your ministry.

A closing illustration will give a picture of the wise balance I hope you leave with. Several years ago I met with Tess, a young woman brought in by her older sister with whom she was temporarily living. Tess had been living with her parents in another part of the country but, due to growing fears and paranoia and the fact that her parents were required to travel abroad for several weeks due to their work, Tess's sister took her in. The same issues their parents noticed continued in this new living situation. Tess firmly believed that the next-door neighbors were breaking into her sister's house when they were not home and stealing some of her belongings. Through the common wall—the house was a duplex—Tess could hear the neighbors whispering and plotting when to break in. However, the sister confirmed that their house was secure and no break-in had occurred. She was unable to hear the nefarious conversations Tess reported. Tess was unable to describe exactly what had gone missing, although this was complicated by the fact that she was in transition and didn't have all her belongings with her at her sister's house. But her sister felt certain that Tess's belongings remained secure.

How did I view Tess? As a young woman with delusions and auditory hallucinations? Possibly schizophrenia? Bipolar disorder? Schizo-affective disorder? Some other diagnostic category? Or did I view her as a scared young woman in an unfamiliar place, deeply distressed that her few precious belongings were being stolen? The answer: Yes! Both! Certainly one priority I had was a consultation with a local psychiatrist to assess her symptoms more fully, which were indeed consistent with psychosis and for which antipsychotic medication might well bring relief. But another priority (which didn't have to wait for a "definitive diagnosis") was to minister to her right in the midst of her fear. Her distress was a real and present experience, even if her perception of the world did not match everyone else's reality. Her fear was genuine even if it was based on a false premise.

In one sense, isn't this the case for all of us when we worry? Our perception of reality at that moment does not include the truth that a sovereign, loving, kind Father is ruling his world and our lives for his glory and our good. At those moments we live as though our existence is fraught with danger at every turn, that we are alone, that the worst that can happen will always happen, and that no one has our backs—all of which are simply not true. So perhaps we are not so different from Tess after all.

This is why the very same reassurances from Scripture that meet me—or you—in our fears had the very same potential to minister to Tess in her particular fears. The task was not to convince her that her fears were unfounded—remember that people are rarely talked out of their delusions and hallucinations—but to take her fear at face value and minister comfort from God's Word in the midst of her anxiety and sense of loss.

And so, after hearing her describe her sadness over the losses she truly felt and her fear about what might additionally be taken from her, we spent time in Luke 12:22-34, making connections with her own experience. As a professing believer, verse 32 was especially meaningful: "'Fear not, little flock, for it is your Father's good pleasure to give you the kingdom.'" We talked about the fact that God had given her a possession that could never be taken away or stolen—his kingdom. She belonged to Jesus and nothing could alter or threaten that reality. She could count on the tender care of her Shepherd, whose joy it was to give Tess "an inheritance that can never perish, spoil or fade" (1 Peter 1:4, NIV).

I only met with Tess a few times before she went back to her parents' home. She did consult with a psychiatrist in my area who prescribed a low dose antipsychotic medication and arranged for follow-up psychiatric care in her parents' region. Tess's psychotic symptoms did not change appreciably during the weeks I met with her, but her framework for addressing her fears became more truth-saturated. Her fear, while still present, was tempered by the reality that God was an ever-present help in times of trouble (Psalm 46:1) and that what truly mattered could not be taken from her. She began to experience a peace that surpassed (her) understanding (Philippians 4:7). This is a brief snapshot of ministry and one that I hope gained further momentum in Tess's home congregation as concerned and caring brothers and sisters came alongside her.

Perhaps you are ministering to someone like Tess right now. Perhaps you have been struggling to make sense of her struggle and to help her in a wise, compassionate, and holistic way. I trust that what I have written bolsters your confidence that Scripture speaks broadly and deeply to those in significant mental distress, whether or not they meet the criteria for a psychiatric diagnosis—and whether or not they take a psychoactive medication. Whatever helping role in the church God has given you, I pray that you have gained encouragement to pursue those struggling with disordered thinking and emotions, knowing that God himself will provide wisdom to care for both the body and soul of those he entrusts to you.

ACKNOWLEDGMENTS

I am thankful for the opportunities I have had through my work at the Christian Counseling and Educational Foundation (CCEF) to develop and hone this material. First and foremost I am grateful for those brothers and sisters who entrusted me with their stories as they came to me for counseling—they have taught me much and have served to winnow the chaff from the wheat in my pastoral counseling and care (an ongoing process, no doubt). I am thankful to have presented this material in a more abbreviated form at the 2011 CCEF National Conference, "Psychiatric Disorders." I have also benefited from thoughtful questions and comments from students as I taught my Counseling and Physiology class each fall. Finally, substantial portions of this book were first published as two articles in *The Journal of Biblical Counseling* (*JBC*): "Listening to Prozac . . . And to the Scriptures: A Primer on Psychoactive Medications," *JBC* 26, no. 1 (2012), 11-22 and "What's in a Name? Understanding Psychiatric Diagnoses," *JBC* 30, no. 1 (2016): 66-93. My thanks to *JBC* editors Kim Monroe and Lauren Whitman who encountered this material in a much less refined form!

My faculty colleagues at CCEF—David Powlison, Ed Welch, Winston Smith (now Priest-in-Charge at St. Anne's Episcopal Church in Abington, PA), Julie Lowe, Todd Stryd, Cecelia Bernhardt, Alasdair Groves, Aaron Sironi, and Monica Kim—have engaged me in many clarifying conversations over the years for which I am profoundly indebted.

I am grateful for the encouragement to write from David Powlison, the Executive Director at CCEF, and Jayne Clark, our chief of staff (and even more grateful for them arranging my weekly responsibilities in such a way that it was actually possible!). The nuanced "third way" approach that is so characteristic of CCEF's ministry is embodied in David's life and ministry and I'm thankful for his mentoring over the years.

Dr. John Applegate has provided exceptional psychiatric care for many in the Philadelphia region over the years. Even more, he has been a wise, godly friend and thoughtful conversation partner. In the midst of a very busy schedule, he provided helpful feedback on earlier drafts of this material including assistance in locating several references from the psychiatric literature. One day, perhaps, I can join him more regularly for some rounds of disc golf!

I am thankful to Mark and Karen Teears at New Growth Press for the opportunity to publish again with them and for Barbara Juliani's gentle persuasion to bring this book to fruition. Finally, I am thankful to Sue Lutz, whose deft editing has made this a better resource for the church. It's been such a pleasure to work with her again.

I remain profoundly thankful that I have two individuals who call me "Dad" every day—my children, Lydia and Luke. I am so proud of them and who they are becoming in Jesus. They help keep me grounded in reality.

Lastly, my wife, Jody, and I will (Lord willing) celebrate twenty years of marriage August 2017. No man could be more blessed.

SCRIPTURE INDEX